Michael Ramsey
as Theologian

Michael Ramsey as Theologian

EDITED BY

Robin Gill and Lorna Kendall

First published in 1995 by
Darton, Longman and Todd Ltd
1 Spencer Court
140–142 Wandsworth High Street
London SW18 4JJ

ISBN 0–232–52081–X

A catalogue record for this book is available
from the British Library

Phototypeset in 11/13pt Caslon Book by Intype, London
Printed and bound in Great Britain
at the University Press, Cambridge

Dedicated to
Lady Joan Ramsey
1910–1995

Contents

Introduction

Michael Ramsey was one of the most theological of modern archbishops of Canterbury. He wrote some 15 theological books and occupied two prestigious theological chairs. He wrote theology even while he was archbishop, and continued writing and thinking about theological issues throughout his retirement. One of his successors, Robert Runcie, wrote in a foreword: 'It is a consolation and an encouragement to a present archbishop that one of his predecessors, after decades spent at the heart of ecclesiastical administration, is able to produce a work like *Be Still and Know*.' Yet there has been comparatively little attention given to Michael Ramsey's theology.

This book attempts to redress this lack of theological attention. All the contributors are theologians with a point of personal contact with Michael Ramsey. The two editors are both grateful for his life and work at many different levels. For Lorna Kendall, formerly Head of Religious Studies at Christ Church College, Canterbury, the Ramseys became deep and personal friends. For Robin Gill, the first holder of the Michael Ramsey Chair of Modern Theology at the University of Kent at Canterbury, the connection with Michael Ramsey lives on in his job. For both of us this has been a labour of love and gratitude. We have dedicated it to our friend, Lady Joan Ramsey, who died on 13 February 1995 but, happily, knew all about this book.

The first contribution is by Rowan Williams, Bishop of Monmouth, and formerly Lady Margaret Professor of Divinity at the University of Oxford. In this article Williams

1

seeks to trace the connections between Michael Ramsey's understanding of theology and his understanding of the Church. Ramsey's *The Gospel and the Catholic Church*, his first and longest book, is central to this analysis. This crucial work was published almost 60 years ago, yet its arguments are still highly informative. Throughout his theology Williams sees Ramsey struggling to understand better both the Church and society at large. He concludes that 'a Church without the thinking and speaking of the underlying nature of its common life is in danger of muffling the critical energy that is in reality always at work in it; a theology without anchorage in the showing of God's life that is the Church's liturgy becomes uncritical in a different way, talkative and bold in its own sophistications'.

James Griffiss, Editor of the *Anglican Theological Review* and formerly William Adams Professor of Systematic Theology at Nashota House, also makes extensive use of Michael Ramsey's *The Gospel and the Catholic Church*. In his essay he seeks to clarify the claim that Ramsey was a 'Catholic' bishop and theologian. Inevitably, this involves Griffiss in a brief examination of some of the different ways that the term 'Catholic' has been used within theology. He cites Ramsey's own claim in *The Gospel and the Catholic Church* that the 'essence of Catholicism' is to be found 'in the unbreakable life to which the sacraments, scriptures, creeds and ministry have never ceased to bear witness'. Apparently unconcerned about the external signs of Catholicism, Ramsey was deeply concerned about what he saw as the fundamentals of Christian faith – and especially creation, incarnation, transfiguration and resurrection. He was a deeply committed 'Catholic' in this sense.

A. M. (Donald) Allchin, formerly Director of the St Theosevia Centre for Christian Spirituality in Oxford and, before that, Canon Residentiary and Librarian of Canterbury Cathedral, writes next on Michael Ramsey and the Orthodox tradition. For Allchin the term 'Orthodoxy' in a sense is substituted for the term 'Catholicity'. It is clear that Michael Ramsey had a long-standing interest in East-

ern orthodoxy. His Catholic and ecumenical nature forced
him to take seriously the divisions between East and West
– whole theology could never be simply Western. He was
always also profoundly conscious of the deep spirituality
of the East, and Allchin rightly draws attention to this
important feature of his theology.

Gordon Wakefield balances the Anglican voices of other
contributors. A distinguished Methodist and ecumenist and
former Principal of Queen's College, Birmingham, he
writes on Michael Ramsey and ecumenical theology.
Ramsey's understanding of 'Catholicism', like that of
F. D. Maurice before him, included a strong commitment
to ecumenism. This most Catholic of archbishops was
also one of our most seriously ecumenical archbishops.
Wakefield traces Ramsey's path from the Congregationalism of his childhood through his commitment as a
student to Anglo-Catholicism and back to his espousal
as Archbishop of Canterbury first of the unsuccessful
Anglican–Methodist Union and then of the successful
Congregational–Presbyterian union. Like other contributors, Wakefield too returns to *The Gospel and the
Catholic Church* to illustrate Ramsey's long-standing
theological and personal commitments in this important
area. From this he picks out another important feature
of Ramsey's ecumenical profile, namely biblical theology
(a type of theology that clearly crossed denominational
boundaries), but finally it is in spirituality and prayer
that Wakefield traces Ramsey's enduring commitment to
ecumenism.

The theme of biblical theology is studied in the article
by John M. Court, Senior Lecturer in Biblical Studies at
the University of Kent at Canterbury. In a sense, biblical
theology is a fashion that has passed, yet it was obviously
crucial to Ramsey's own theology. Without being formally
a biblical scholar he was nevertheless a theologian who
was deeply informed at every stage by the Bible. More than
that, biblical theology sought enduring themes within the
Bible which could be used in theology in the modern

world. Court shows how Ramsey sought such themes in many of his books, including *The Resurrection of Christ*, *The Glory of God and the Transfiguration of Christ*, *Jesus and the Living Past*, and finally in *Be Still and Know*. Court argues that Ramsey's skill 'was to maintain a strict equilibrium between history and theology even at a time when the reliance upon history was being seriously questioned'. Furthermore, Ramsey 'offered a mode of reconciliation between academic and spiritual concerns'. While recognizing these real strengths Court argues that Ramsey's biblical theology also exceeded available evidence and exaggerated the distinctiveness of biblical themes. Sadly, this is now one of the more anachronistic elements in Ramsey's theology.

Kenneth Leech, Maurice Reckitt Urban Fellow and priest-in-charge of St Botolph's Church, Aldgate, and formerly Director of the Runnymede Trust, writes about Michael Ramsey's social theology. He too starts with Ramsey's *The Gospel and the Catholic Church*, and sees within its critique of liberal theology the seeds of Ramsey's social theology. For Ramsey gospel, Church and sacraments were inseparable, allowing Christians to take the world seriously without being accommodated to its dominant but passing values. Depicting Ramsey's position as a 'materialistic spirituality' and as an heir to the legacy of F. D. Maurice, Leech places him firmly in a radical social incarnational and sacramental tradition. Leech's analysis offers many insights into Ramsey's response to such ethical issues as nuclear deterrence and homosexual reform and, most crucially, the race and immigration debates of the 1960s. Although clearly an admirer of Ramsey's social theology, Leech finally concludes that it 'was marked by the very transcendent character which he had criticised in Barth . . . abstracted from the mess and concreteness of life on earth'.

Lorna Kendall's article on pastoral theology, however, reveals another side to Michael Ramsey's theology. Manifestly a pastor throughout his ministry, he was also deeply concerned to make his fellow clergy think and read more theology. Ramsey, she argues, 'thought it to be of the highest importance that the clergy should read and pass on to their congregations the fruit of their study'. In the course of his diocesan letters he recommended or reviewed some 150 books, sometimes at considerable length. Using the rich and largely untapped source of Ramsey's diocesan letters, Kendall seeks to outline some of the theological themes that emerge time and again. The themes of transfiguration, priesthood and prayer were crucial both to Ramsey's own pastoral ministry and to the ministry which he sought to encourage in others.

Louis Weil, Professor of Liturgy at the Church Divinity School of the Pacific, Berkeley, California, and formerly of Nashota House, focuses upon liturgy in Ramsey's theology. For Weil the 'importance of liturgy for Ramsey is always rooted in its power to manifest the nature of the Church as the people of God to fulfil their vocation in the world'. Like James Griffiss he notes that Ramsey's 'Catholicism' did not lie in external signs or acts, but in a profound sense of the 'incompleteness' of all existing Christian traditions. *The Gospel and the Catholic Church* is once again the primary theological source from which Weil draws. The second half of Weil's article is concerned with Ramsey's attitudes towards initiation, eucharist and ordination – signs of 'God's action towards humankind and the role of personal faith as the necessary subjective response to God's action for us'. All these signs, however, are always set by Ramsey in a securely ecclesiological context. Liturgy and sacraments are essentially the liturgy and sacraments of the Church.

George Carey, Archbishop of Canterbury and formerly a theological college principal, re-examines the *Honest to God* controversy and Michael Ramsey's role within it. In later life Ramsey himself tended to look back on this controversy as a personal failure. There can be little doubt that he remained fond of John Robinson and regretted some of the things said and written while the controversy was raging. George Carey draws upon private correspondence still held at Lambeth Palace and is able as a result to paint a fuller picture than has been possible hitherto of some of the theological and ecclesiological factors involved in the debate. Particularly interesting is Ramsey's deep concern that Robinson should not be prosecuted as a 'heretic' within the Church's courts. Ramsey was also concerned about responsible leadership and about the proper place for freedom of thought within the Church. As a result of his analysis of this controversy, the present Archbishop of Canterbury reflects upon the present-day role of bishops as teachers of the faith: 'the episode reveals the problems that can arise if bishops are not in the habit of anticipating contentious issues, of sharing their thoughts and then acting collegially by working through their differences together'.

Finally, Robin Gill concludes with a theological speculation. Supposing for a moment that both Michael Ramsey and Eric Mascall had lived to the age of ninety, he wonders how they might have responded to the *Honest to God* of the 1990s – namely, Anthony Freeman's *God in Us*. Neither book can claim to be a particularly distinguished contribution to theology (both are highly derivative and, in places, poorly argued), yet they have both provoked considerable debate outside the theological world. Gill speculates that although both Ramsey and Mascall would have thoroughly disliked the book, nevertheless their attacks upon it would have been quite different. Mascall would surely have dissected its arguments with considerable gusto and ridiculed it as yet another example of the secularization of Christian theology. Ramsey would probably have approached it with a more generous orthodoxy – with an affirmation of the notion of 'God in us' but a gentle insistence upon 'Us in God' as well.

Perhaps we can finish with a more personal note. Commissioning the various essays for this book has reminded us both of the enormous affection which still surrounds the memory of Michael Ramsey. We hope that the essays please others as much as they have pleased us in producing them.

1   Theology and the Churches

Rowan Williams

'Christian theology is not only a detached exercise of the Christian intellect; it is the life of the one Body in which Truth is both thought out and lived out.'[1]

'Under modern conditions I think a theologian has got to be a heretic. The relation between religious belief and modern culture is so extreme you have to be innovative and exploratory. You have to be all the things that Michael Ramsey abhorred.'[2]

Two radically different judgements on the nature of theology, one from Ramsey himself, one from the doyen of contemporary Anglican 'heretics', Don Cupitt. How are such judgements formed, and how should both Church and academy think now about theology? What I want to suggest here is that how you think about theology, how you make your judgements as to what kind of an enterprise it is, how you conceive its relation to the life of the churches, actually depends, in the long run, on how you are thinking about the Church in the first place. This may sound a bit circular: what we say about theology depends on our theology of the Church. However, I have in mind not so much some sort of 'given' doctrine of the Church but rather the underlying, imperfectly voiced assumptions as to the sort of thing the Church is – which, in turn, reflect the underlying assumptions as to the nature of what (if anything) is done for us in the events of Jesus' life and death. Ramsey, above all in that abiding classic, *The Gospel and the Catholic Church*, stands within a broad trend in Anglican, Roman Catholic and Orthodox thinking in this century which seeks to articulate one particular sense of what the Church is; a sense which is currently much in eclipse in two of those traditions and often rather distorted in the third; a sense, too, which is obscured by both self-consciously traditionalist and self-consciously liberal theologians at present. The perspective expressed by Don Cupitt's remarks, on the other hand, expresses a sense of the Church's identity that is substantially and, I think, irreconcilably different. The question we are left with in investigating these two approaches is whether, finally, we have to stand with either Ramsey or Cupitt; whether the sense Ramsey works with is part of the necessary common sense of the Church, without which theology, worship, ecumenism, whatever, are going to be empty.

Ramsey's first book was far from uncontroversial when it appeared in 1936.[3] It was regarded with dismay by many in Ramsey's former (and future) university as another example of the malign influence of foreign irrationalism – the new Protestant orthodoxy of Barth, especially – just as much as an example of ecclesiastical rigidity: *theologians* ought not to waste their time writing about liturgy and things like that.[4] It is perhaps easier now than, say, twenty years ago to understand the depth of feeling that could pervade debates about the place and authority of revelation in theology at a time when the faltering responses of classical liberalism to the horrors of war and totalitarianism had prompted a good many to despair of any kind of common rationality as a tool, let alone a source, for theology. Today a similar debate continues, with some of the same intensity of feeling, over whether theology has a 'rationality' proper to itself in a world where, once again, the resources of liberalism are running thin; but now the situation is further complicated by the intellectual importance of a 'post-modern' milieu that is sceptical of *any* universalizing intellectual projects, and at times seems to relish the prospect of a tribalizing of intellectual life.[5] Ramsey's book represents what was to become a more and more powerful and popular option in certain Anglican circles over the decade that followed its first publication. It takes up the challenges posed by his mentor Edwyn Hoskyns both in the latter's own work and in his translation of Barth's second commentary on Romans:[6] challenges that might be summarized as forcing upon the rather comfortable world of Anglican philosophical theology the imperative of rediscovering a theology of the cross. The very first chapter of *The Gospel and the Catholic Church* (entitled 'The Passion and the Church Today') sets the tone very clearly: the problems of the Church, not least problems of reunion between Christians, cannot be met, or even intelligently thought about, unless it is recognized that the Church exists because of the death and resurrection of Jesus, and that any project in which the Church approaches more nearly to 'becoming what it is' (not Ramsey's phrase) involves sacrifice, dispossession. All projects and ideals, theological, spiritual, intellectual, social, must go into the melting-pot under the imperative of the cross of God incarnate. It is no accident that, in later chapters,[7] some of Ramsey's most impassioned writing is devoted to Luther – not such a very common bedfellow for a Catholic Anglican divine (then or now).[8]

This alignment with the demands of the cross brought with it a consciously rhetorical and often paradoxical style. It was to be echoed in other writers of the same tendency: think of the extremism, what one commentator has called the 'brutality', of Donald MacKinnon's early theological essays, which undoubtedly owe much to Hoskyns and Ramsey.[9] The vision seems to dictate a strong note of extremism, indeed, of what the same commentator has called 'impossibilism':[10] the Church, in common with the whole redemptive process, does not exist as the fruit of human endeavour, which is shown time and again by the bloody collapse of 'civilized' rationality to be incapable of

attaining anything that is lastingly healing. Thus the
Church cannot be reformed by human effort and ingen-
uity, any more than sin can be eradicated by good will.
We must hear the gospel of the Incarnation as a summons
to self-abandonment before all else, not as a reassuring
endorsement of the best we can humanly do. In the light
of this, it is odd to see Ramsey, here as elsewhere, giving
so much house room to F. D. Maurice, whose theological
interest in what a later German generation was to reject
as 'creation ordinances' independent of the gospel (the
organic structures of nation, community and family) seems
so much at odds with the theology of the cross that dominates most of Ramsey's first book. Indeed, the passages in
which Ramsey attempts to show that Maurice too sees the
disruptive cross at the centre of theology[11] fall some way
short of a persuasive argument: Maurice certainly stresses
the need for the Church to put the atonement at the heart
of its preaching, but is more interested in the *complete-
ness* of what has been achieved in the sacrifice of Christ
than in the Christian appropriation of the way of the
cross.[12]

If we ask, however, why Ramsey should have found
Maurice so sympathetic (and it was not an affinity he ever
forswore),[13] the answer in fact tells us much about the
central and controlling vision that animates *The Gospel
and the Catholic Church*, and thus about what Ramsey
thought theology was. Maurice is profoundly concerned
(as few if any theologians of his or Ramsey's generation
were) with the centrality of *trinitarian* theology; and he
also (again in a way not easy to parallel in other writers
of the age) grants a place of the highest significance in
theological method to the language of the Church's public
worship. In short, Maurice was concerned to understand
the Church's life as something in which *the nature of God
was made manifest*; and this was close enough to Ramsey's animating enthusiasms to make of Maurice an ally
against both the liberalism he and Maurice rejected so
passionately, and the conservatism that saw the Church

as fundamentally a divinely organized institution, whose structures were given under law. If we now read Maurice a little more suspiciously,[14] noting the hierarchical assumptions that sit comfortably unquestioned in his social thought and his theological positivism about the state as divinely instituted, we should remember that in Ramsey's day critical discussion of Maurice – indeed, discussion of any kind regarding his work – was in its infancy. For most of those who bothered to read him at all, he had something of the same liberating impact as he obviously had in Ramsey's case: he was heard, rightly, as a voice breaking through some sterile oppositions between Protestant and Catholic loyalties.

This third way opened up the minds of many Anglicans to a perspective that was beginning to appear in continental Catholicism and was being introduced into the ecumenical scene largely by émigré Russian writers.[15] It is essentially the vision of the Church as 'epiphany': what matters about the Church is not a system of ideas as such (though doctrine and dogma have their place) nor the structure of an organization competent to deliver authoritative judgements and to require obedience (though order is important in its proper context), but what the bare fact of the Church *shows*. *The Gospel and the Catholic Church* sets out first to determine the shape of divine action (gift, sacrifice, the creation of a qualitatively new human fellowship) and then to demonstrate how doctrine and discipline in the Catholic tradition make present and tangible the pattern of divine action. In an unusually sharp couple of sentences on Calvin and the weaknesses of his theology of the Christian community,[16] Ramsey expresses very clearly what he believes matters most for the Church:

> For Calvin, however, the Church is rather utilitarian. It is not perceived as the glow of Christ's incarnate presence; it is the policeman sent to protect the Christian life by commands and prohibitions. Here is discipline, without the sense of union with the death and life of Christ which gives disci-

13

pline its meaning; here is order, without the sense of the wondrous historical and apostolic race which gives order its meaning.

I suspect that Ramsey is really doing what he generally says should not be done – treating a theology of ministry as a theology of the Church, castigating Calvin for not retaining the sense of Catholic order in his functionalist remoulding of the Christian ministry. Others would want to defend Calvin's *overall* theology of the worshipping community as far closer to Ramsey's ideal. However, the point is that Ramsey has already elaborated at length his reasons for believing that the traditional Catholic order is not an alien superstructure imposed on a 'message', but is actually the *language* in which that message is communicable in its fullness. Furthermore, he does, in effect, grant in his earlier pages about the medieval Church that Calvin and others could be forgiven for missing the point in the climate of their own day.

Fundamentally, however, the Church *is* the message. There is no cluster of ideas or ideals that can be abstracted from the life of the Church and passed on in some sort of neutral medium; to belong in the Church is to know what God wants you to know, because it is to live as God wants you to live. But this is where we need to read carefully. Put as baldly as that – God wants you to belong to the Church – Ramsey's vision is not only unattractive, it could be read as a call to conformism or submission to an institutional authority. This is what it would mean if the Church were here being defined as a society devoted to promoting certain kinds of behaviour or ideas as specified by an expert élite or governing caste; and much of the tragedy of the Church's history derives from the fact that this is exactly how the Church has appeared at various times. Ramsey has hard words for the doctrine of papal authority because it defines the unity of the Church in terms of a unity of 'executive' power: there is one supreme legitimate source for imperatives in faith and morals, and belonging in the Church is equivalent to submission to this.[17] Not much better is what Ramsey sees as the Protestant distortion that appears to understand unity in terms either of what can be enforced by the biblically educated pastors of the community (as in his characterization of Calvin already quoted) or of shared feelings.[18] But the true Church does not exist for the sake of advancing something other than its own integrity – whether it is a system of authoritative teaching or a set of sentiments. It is first and foremost the epiphany of God's action, especially God's action in the paschal events, and so too of God's nature. It exists to radiate the glory of God.

This can only be seriously maintained, of course, if we allow that the Church is what it is visibly and tangibly in one specific context – the Eucharist. This is not an arbitrary stipulation. If what it is to be a Christian is to be 'in Christ', the community of Christians is what it is only in so far as it is in Christ, united with Christ's divine action. It is itself where human beings renounce their private and protected selfhoods 'in a death like his', so that their self-emptying mirrors the self-emptying of God the Word in Jesus' life and death. Considered as a narrative about human biographies, this process of self-emptying is always going to be flawed and incomplete, vulnerable to corruption and failure. Yet the Church is not, in the New Testament, simply a project initiated by Jesus and struggling to achieve its destiny; it exists in its fullness, it is already the community of those who are holy and who bear the identity of Christ. Thus the Church is itself precisely where it is transparent to the divine action – which means that the Church is itself in the sacraments. Here the diversity of human biographies is traced back to its source in the act of God, and the diversity of Christian biographies is traced back to the one unrepeatable event of Good Friday and Easter; the Church's unity is 'in a real sense a sharing in those events'[19] and so in the single coherent divine action that eternally underlies and makes sense of the paschal story. Baptism inaugurates the reality

15

of a life that can be transparent to God; but the rite that *manifests* all this repeatedly, publicly, corporately is the Eucharist. Here 'It is still the Messiah who gives thanks and breaks bread'; and the Eucharistic liturgy 'is not only the most important of a series of rites, but the divine act into which all prayers and praises are drawn'.[20] In such a context, the ordained ministry of the Church is simply what serves to show the full meaning of the sacramental assembly: that it is united in time to the events of Easter and that it lives always by a life that is not and could not be restricted to a local or sectional or national context. The Catholic ministry is a mark of the kenotic structure of the Church's life, the fundamental truth that no person or specific community lives of, by or for itself.

Such is the apostolic function as the New Testament seems to envisage it;[21] and this, Ramsey argues eloquently in the sixth chapter of *The Gospel and the Catholic Church*, is exactly what episcopacy now expresses in the Catholic Church. The bishop or his deputy presiding at the assembly of the Church in order to let the Messiah act, in order to bring the prayers of the Christian people into unity with the self-offering in time and eternity of Christ the High Priest,[22] is part of the way in which the Church, simply by being what it is, communicates the glory of God. The presence of the ordained is not dictated by juridical requirements or by some theory of occult powers granted only to the clergy. They are there presiding in the assembly in order to show something – the unity of the Church in the cross and resurrection of Jesus. Without the apostolic ministry, the problem is not a defect of 'validity' in the usual Catholic sense but a defect of clarity and intelligibility in the symbolic communication of the gospel of God. The liturgy becomes a performance of a choral work with one whole vocal part missing – not quite *Hamlet* without the Prince, but the harmony without the sopranos, perhaps.

This is one of the points where Ramsey is probably closest to some of his Orthodox friends and mentors. It is noteworthy that such discussion as there is in the Russian Orthodox works Ramsey would have read on the subject of ordained ministry concentrates heavily on the 'epiphanic' role of the clergy,[23] not on their power of rule or their pastoral or teaching task. If you want to know what clergy are for, do not start with pragmatic considerations, the jobs you would like clergy to do in running things or providing 'leadership' (not a word you would expect Ramsey to relish in a book focusing so closely on the priority of the cross); start with the *picture* of an assembly that in its formal structure and its disposition of responsibilities and its language, gesture and process draws you towards a contemplative understanding of the act of God in cross and resurrection and in the eternal love by which God is God. You could, I think, quite reasonably ask of Ramsey's model (as some have asked of Orthodox models) whether *this* Church exists, practically speaking, between celebrations of the Eucharist, or even whether the ordained should have any specific responsibilities other than the conduct of the epiphanic liturgy. I suspect that Ramsey's answer to that would probably be in elaborating what it is to be given the sort of 'guardianship' of the Church's unity in the cross that is spelled out in the chapters on order in general and bishops in particular. It is also, of course, given concretely and unforgettably in his masterpiece of practical pastoral theology, *The Christian Priest Today*; but that takes us into rather different territory.

Now the point of this brief overview of the themes of Ramsey's first book is to indicate what is being taken for granted in the comment on theology with which this paper began. We could sum this up by saying that it depends on a distinctive view of truth itself, truth as *appropriate relation to reality* at every level. We habitually assume that the only appropriate relation that matters is the supposed correspondence of words to things; but this is increasingly inadequate both as a theological and as a philosophical foundation, or so we have been told by a good many recent

17

writers.[24] Ramsey, in his ninth chapter, elaborates what he describes as the 'biblical' model of truth: truth is 'a quality of the living God in action', and thus appears as 'God's saving plan as He rules in history'.[25] Consequently, we know it in so far as we are taken into the shape and movement of that action – which means in turn that it cannot be apprehended without repentance and transfiguration. This is how what scripture calls 'wisdom' is imparted, giving to us the light in which we are to interpret the whole range of our human environment.[26] Yet again, Ramsey is best read alongside some of the major Orthodox theologians of the century: Florovsky, certainly, but more recently John Zizioulas, who has developed the theme of the inseparability of 'Truth and Communion' (the title of a major essay that deserves a paper to itself).[27] Here we find a stress not so much on the characteristically sub-Barthian idea of the truth as the act of God which appears in Ramsey, but on truth as itself that indestructible life that is open to us when we cease to live as private and self-determining individuals and enter the communion of the Church's life, which is also the communion of God's own personal life-in-relation. And, since Zizioulas links this very directly to the Eucharist,[28] the parallel with Ramsey is very close indeed.

The role of theology, then, is strictly unintelligible in such a context if it once ceases to be reflection on *relations* that have been established by something other than an individual intellect – the relation of our words to God's act and our *acts* to God's act that is imparted in the liturgy and made possible by the incarnation, death and resurrection of the Word, and then the relation of Christian persons to one another in a community that is never simply an association of individuals with interests in common. The norms and limits of theology are thus set not by the decree of an external authority (and we could look again here at Ramsey's hostile pages on papal authoritarianism) but by the logic of these relations. That is to say, theology would simply stop being itself if it

abandoned the belief that in Jesus God had acted to recon-
struct the bonds that unite humanity and connect it with
the source of divine life; or even if it redefined the Eucharist as an aid to individual devotion or a ceremony expressive of deep feelings of human solidarity. A theologian who
went down such paths would not be doing bad or even
heretical theology; she or he would not be doing theology
at all, merely a no doubt respectable and disciplined and
serious form of independent religious reflection on the
social patterns of a community whose origins and meaning
could be adequately accounted for in straightforwardly historical terms. If this is right, then for Ramsey – as, I think,
for Hooker[29] – there cannot but be some grey areas in the
detail of dogmatic teaching (not least about the structures
of Church and ministry); but what remains non-negotiable
is the central complex of commitments which depend on
a belief that God acts to renew the divine image, in person
and community, through Jesus. Ramsey's initially hostile
response to *Honest to God*, a response which he later
regretted somewhat, has about it a sense of disquiet at the
dismissal not of insupportable ideas but of deep-rooted
idioms of prayer.[30] While Ramsey undoubtedly found it
hard to see exactly what doctrine of God and Christ John
Robinson was advancing, his chief anxiety was to do with
what he clearly thought to be Robinson's 'tone-deafness'
as to the language of piety. It is not fair to say, as has
been said,[31] that Ramsey was wholly unreceptive to new
theological ideas, though his reading was not much less
restricted than that of most bishops tends to become after
a few years (shades of the prison-house . . .). He did, however, take it for granted that there was a focus to Christian
belief and practice which, precisely because it was not a
matter of conceptual structures, but a multiple and elusive
sense of the divine action in Jesus and the worshipping
community, was simply not vulnerable to intellectual or
cultural fashion – and to speak or write as if it were would
be to stop doing theology, to turn to one's own agenda
as the subject-matter of religious reflection. In so far as

19

Ramsey thought again about *Honest to God*, it was surely because he recognized, as have several generations of readers, that the conceptually troubled waters at the surface of the book conceal a commitment as strong in many ways as Ramsey's own to the vision of a new humanity in Christ, realized in the Eucharistic assembly.

Yet this particular case focuses the kind of difficulty felt even by the most sympathetic contemporary reader of Ramsey. If you begin by taking for granted the historic community, liturgy and hierarchy of the Church, if this is to be the context and the test for all theological utterance, are we not faced with the danger that theology becomes the self-justification of the Church, an ideology of ecclesiastical power? The account of the role of bishops in the Church, for instance, is eloquent and even compelling in terms of epiphany and symbolism; but we must surely also be aware of what it means and has always meant in terms of the concrete exercise of power. Does the history of ecclesiastical hierarchy allow us to speak so serenely about what is made manifest in the Eucharistic assembly? We have been urged all too often in recent years to reread much of early Christian history as a history of struggles for ideological dominance;[32] and if theology is defined as reflection on the epiphany of God's character in the hierarchically organized assembly, it will be in danger of burying a great deal of history. It might be just as theological (or even *more* theological) to reflect on the history of struggle, power and exclusion in the Church. The theologies that now come from those who have experienced this history of exclusion, women especially, ought surely to have some claim to count as authentic, a 'living out of Truth' in the life of the Body.

This is, I believe, a fair objection, as it is to some styles of Orthodox theology. A faith in which historical narration is fundamental can hardly afford to conceal its own history when it reflects on its nature and calling. Ramsey, of course, does engage with some aspects of the history of the Church in the last few chapters of *The Gospel and the*

Catholic Church, but there is a tendency here for the discussion to slip into a kind of intellectual history dominated by 'ideal types' (as witness his account of Calvinism, already referred to), and innocent of contextual problems (as in the discussion of F. D. Maurice). He was, of course, writing at a time when this particular kind of ideological suspiciousness was by no means a regular part of the intellectual historian's equipment. Certainly, Ramsey enlarges at length upon the 'perversions' of Western Christianity in the medieval period, but this is always in terms of a decline from the golden age of the Fathers, which is not itself subjected to critical historical analysis. It cannot be denied that all this constitutes a weakness in the style of theology advocated and embodied in *The Gospel*. When all this is granted, however, there is a crucially important counter-point to be made. If the theologies that emerge from the experience of the victimized and excluded, the theologies that deploy suspicion and ideological critique, are to be in any sense *theology*, not just the expression of an assortment of resentments, they are bound to work with a governing critical model of what the Body might be. They become a manifestation of the life of the Body as a *thinking* life to the extent that they continue to pose as the ultimate critical point of reference a system of relations between persons established by the events of revelation – that is, by the history of Israel and Jesus. Without this, a purportedly critical theology can become an uncritical deployment of whatever are supposed to be the most obvious and socially accessible models of the good life at any given time. What I called earlier in this essay 'the faltering responses of classical liberalism' to the crisis of public values in the 1930s are as inadequate now as then.

In a much-quoted and haunting phrase,[33] Ramsey speaks of what the Catholic Church 'learns and re-learns in humiliation': 'Catholicism always stands before the church door at Wittenberg to read the truth by which she is created and by which also she is judged.' Perhaps we best understand the critical resources of Ramsey's theology in the light of a remark like this. The Church must always be looking at and appropriating its own historical failure; in so far as 'Wittenberg' represents (for Ramsey) a moment when the Catholic tradition is challenged to acknowledge its failure, it articulates a principle of basic theological importance. The Church lives under judgement: its empirical condition is always to be thought through, tested in the light of the reality to which its existence is supposed to bear witness. While the normal manifestation of that reality is the sacramental life of the Eucharistic assembly, there are times when this has to be activated in the imagination and consciousness of the Church by history itself, by moments of rupture and protest. But *if* the Church has actually been paying attention to the substance of its sacramental life, it ought to be able to interpret such historical moments correctly, and so to 'learn in humiliation'.

In other words, I think Ramsey is granting implicitly that what might seem like a disturbingly seamless and epiphanic model of the Church, timelessly showing forth in its liturgy and hierarchy the mystery of God's nature, will not tell us the whole story. If we understand what it means to enact in worship the pattern of God's kenosis, the costly mutuality that is established by the death and resurrection of Jesus, and the universal horizon of God's work in Christ, we should be on the watch constantly for the kind of ideological bondage that threatens to take over a Church-based or Church-focused theology. But the liturgy is, humanly speaking, administered and actualized by fallible human agents, who are all enmeshed in relations other than those of the redeemed community, and who thus constantly introduce such alien patterns into the Church, even when presiding at the Eucharistic assembly, the eschatological congregation of God's people bonded in charity. This is why it will not do to have a theology of ordained ministry that is entirely based on their epiphanic role, however important it may be to redress the balance against managerial and governmental models. The Church may be perfectly the Church at the Eucharist, but its life is not exhausted in the Eucharist: there is a life that is always struggling to realize outside the 'assembly' what the assembly shows forth.[34] In that context, theology requires the angry and sometimes disruptive gestures of history, requires the naming of 'humiliation', in order to recognize the prophetic import of what it does in worship, especially when even worship in its presentation or structure at any one time may speak of injustices or betrayals of the gospel (as when the ordained ministry speaks of one or another kind of social exclusion, when ceremonial speaks of anxiety or servility, when language evokes alienating or oppressive images).

Ramsey, in short, is difficult to claim for either reaction or radicalism as normally understood. But – to return to the antithesis with which I began this essay – he would not, I think, have seen the point of defining the theologian's task as necessarily heretical. The tension for him is not between 'religious belief' and 'modern culture' as two systems of thought, but rather between the form of corporate human life realized through Christ and the Spirit in the Eucharistic assembly and all other forms of human sociality. Furthermore, this is a tension (not, of course, an absolute opposition) that is not to be resolved by thinking, by conceptual readjustments. Where there is a crisis of plausibility, where the Church is manifestly alienated from the currents of contemporary reflection and perception, the exploratory religious thinking of an individual is *not* of necessity the way to overcome it. In Ramsey's frame of reference, what needs doing is a mutual probing by Church and not-Church, a reciprocal testing of honesty and resource, which cannot be reduced to a programme of revisionism. For a theologian to try to test the integrity of his or her world of religious discourse requires a fundamental commitment to that world as deserving of attention, as having depths worth sounding, even when the surface language is muddled or obscure, just as much as it demands an attention to the forms of social construction and the cultural voices that currently prevail. It demands a belief that the life of the Body can appropriately be 'thought', and not only lived unreflectively or uncritically. Yet this in turn takes it for granted that there is some 'pre-understanding' of the distinctiveness of the Body itself – which can only be nurtured by the distinctive common practices of the Body, by worship and the daily struggles for holiness and justice in human affairs. When Bonhoeffer, in his unforgettable letter to his godson of May 1944,[35] spoke of the failures of religious words to transform the world, he envisaged a time when Christian self-awareness would have to remain content with 'prayer and righteous action', living in expectancy of a rebirth of words gifted with presence and power. Ramsey's style of theologizing is about as different as could be from Bonhoeffer's, but, to the extent that Ramsey stresses the Church's need to learn in 'humiliation', to be brought to silence before what has created it, he may point us to the same place. Some things must be shown not spoken, or shown before spoken; or the speaking has to be absorbed again and again into the showing. A Church without the thinking and speaking of the underlying nature of its common life is in danger of muffling the critical energy that is in reality always at work in it; a theology without anchorage in the showing of God's life that is the Church's liturgy becomes uncritical in a different way, talkative and bold in its own sophisti-cations. To say that Ramsey's is the only rationale, finally, for a theology that does not turn into religious phenomen-ology is not a recipe for repetitious ideology and obedient intellectual idleness in the Church; simply an acknow-ledgement that, if there is anything at all to be said for understanding the gospel as a gift, and, more specifically, a gift in the form of a remaking of human bonds, theology will always be stumbling to keep up with something prior. That is both its privilege and its cross, articulating (from the theologian's own experience in the Church) the 'learning in humiliation', learning in the failure and impotence of formulae, that returns the Church to its source.

Notes

1. Michael Ramsey, *The Gospel and the Catholic Church* (London, 1936) p. 124. Henceforth *GCC*.
2. Don Cupitt, quoted in Michael De-la-Noy, *Michael Ramsey: A Portrait* (London, 1990), p. 99.
3. For reactions, see Owen Chadwick, *Michael Ramsey. A Life* (Oxford, 1990), pp. 48–50. For a very positive appraisal of *GCC*'s strengths in the context of its time, compare the brief remarks of Adrian Hastings, *A History of English Christianity, 1920–1985* (London, 1986), p. 261.
4. Readers may recall Dean Inge's reported comment when asked if he was interested in liturgy ('No. Neither do I collect postage stamps'), or A. C. Headlam's alleged judgement that, of all academic disciplines, those that most sapped the intellect were Hebrew and liturgiology.
5. John Milbank's *Theology and Social Theory*, (Oxford, 1990), represents the most systematic and original contribution to this debate from the theological world of late. See also the special issues of *New Blackfriars* (June 1992) and *Modern Theology* (October 1992) devoted to Milbank's book. For a wider spread of essays on religion and post-modernism, see Philippa Berry and Andrew Wernick (eds), *Shadow of Spirit. Religion and Post-modernism* (London, 1992).
6. For an excellent memoir of Hoskyns and a list of his works, see the introduction by Gordon Wakefield to the posthumously edited *Crucifixion–Resurrection. The Pattern of the Theology and Ethics of the New Testament*, E. C. Hoskyns and F. N. Davey (London, 1981), pp. 27–81, and the bibliography, pp. 369–72.
7. *GCC*, pp. 169–71, 180, 181–93.
8. In this respect, he stands in sharp contrast to Gregory Dix, in some respects a kindred theological spirit; see, for example, *The Shape of the Liturgy* (London, 1945), pp. 629–36, notably p. 636 ('Luther furnishes curious parallels with Adolf Hitler . . .'). The Methodist Gordon Rupp, whose earliest excursions into Luther scholarship were stimulated by comments comparable to those of Dix, was largely responsible for presenting to the British theological

public a more balanced picture of Luther; in the 1960s, he and Ramsey shared a commitment to the ill-fated cause of Anglican–Methodist reunion. There would be an interesting essay to be written on the parallels between these two remarkable figures in whom the glib oppositions of Catholic and Protestant seemed to be overcome.

9. Richard Roberts, 'Theological rhetoric and moral passion in the light of MacKinnon's "Barth" ', in Kenneth Surin (ed.), *Christ, Ethics and Tragedy. Essays in Honour of Donald MacKinnon* (Cambridge, 1989), pp. 1–14 (e.g. p. 12).

10. Ibid., p. 12 ('an ecclesiological impossibilism grounded at least in part in an appropriation of dialectical theology').

11. *GCC*, pp. 210ff.

12. Despite the quotation on p. 212 ('The death of Christ is actually, literally, the death of you and me'), Maurice seems more concerned to make a point about our recognition of the illusoriness of the isolated self than to elaborate a pedagogy of the cross. We should also note the difference between Maurice's and Barth's repudiations of 'religion'. Maurice rejects 'religion' as a separate sphere of culture and polity, Barth as the human attempt to domesticate God in culture and polity.

13. Some of the material from *GCC* is reproduced pretty much as it stands in Michael Ramsey (ed. Dale Coleman), *The Anglican Spirit* (London, 1991), pp. 69–77.

14. See, for example, David Nicholls and Rowan Williams, *Politics and Theological Identity* (London, 1984).

15. *GCC* has two references to Georges Vasilievich Florovsky on ecclesiology; the middle 1930s marked the beginnings of Florovsky's influence in the ecumenical movement, and of his regular visits to English and Scottish theological institutions. He met Ramsey during the latter's time at Lincoln, and they continued friends. See Andrew Blane (ed.), *Georges Florovsky: Russian Intellectual, Orthodox Churchman* (New York, 1993), p. 69, with n. 81 on p. 186, and n. 230 on p. 205.

16. *GCC*, p. 197.

17. Ibid., p. 172.

18. Ibid., pp. 198–201; and see p. 120 on the mirror image of the failures of Catholicism and Protestantism.

19. Ibid., p. 28.

20. Ibid., p. 118.

21. Ibid., p. 73.

22. There is a venerable Anglican tradition behind this, perhaps most eloquently set out in Jeremy Taylor's *The Worthy Communicant*; see, for example, the text quoted in (ed. Thomas K. Carroll), *Jeremy Taylor: Selected Works* (New York/Mahwah, NJ, 1990), pp. 209ff.

23. In addition to Florovsky's work, Ramsey would probably have read Sergei Bulgakov, *The Orthodox Church* (London, 1935); ch. 3 of this work sets out a theology of 'hierarchy' in terms of the 'charismatic power' to transmit the grace of the sacraments, quite distinct from any power to rule over the laity as subjects, which would be destructive of the sense of interdependent charisms in the one Church. In addition, the closeness of Ramsey's vision to that of John Zizioulas, in more recent Orthodox thought, is striking; see, in particular, chs 5 and 6 of Zizioulas's *Being as Communion* (London, 1985).

24. Two relevant (though very different) books in this connection are Donald Davidson's influential collection, *Inquiries into Truth and Interpretation* (Oxford, 1984), and Fergus Kerr, *Theology after Wittgenstein* (Oxford, 1986). Both defend varieties of realism (language has a relation to what is not language, and is in some significant measure determined by what is not language) while demonstrating that a theory of language as the naming of discrete lumps of experienced reality is philosophically unsustainable.

25. *GCC*, p. 121.

26. Ibid., pp. 121–4.

27. Ch. 2 of *Being as Communion* (above, n. 23); cf. Florovsky's essay, 'Revelation, Philosophy, and Theology' (originally published in German in 1931), in *Creation and Redemption*, vol. 3 of the Collected Works of Georges Florovsky (Belmont, Mass., 1976), pp. 21–40.

28. *Being as Communion*, pp. 114–22.

29. See the present writer's essay, 'Richard Hooker: Philosopher, Anglican, Contemporary', in the forthcoming collection of papers from the 1993 Folger Library conference to celebrate the fourth centenary of the opening books of Hooker's *Laws* and the completion of the new Folger Library edition of the text; to be published by Cambridge University Press (ed. A. S. McGrade).

30. For the text of Ramsey's remarks in his presidential address to the Convocation of Canterbury in May 1963, in which he expressed some criticism of *Honest to God*, see Eric James, *A Life of Bishop John A. T. Robinson: Scholar,*

Pastor, Prophet (London, 1987), pp. 120–1. His booklet, *Image Old and New*, published a little earlier, had set out more sympathetically and fully some of his reactions.

31. Michael De-la-Noy, op. cit., pp. 100, 194–6, quoting a variety of contemporary theologians.

32. See, for example, the very powerful and often moving works of Graham Shaw, *The Cost of Authority* (London, 1983), and *God in our Hands* (London, 1987); and studies of the patristic period such as those of Elaine Pagels (*The Gnostic Gospels* (London, 1980); *Adam, Eve and the Serpent* (London, 1988)).

33. *GCC*, p. 180.

34. I have tried to elaborate this a little in 'Imagining the Kingdom: some questions for Anglican worship today', in Kenneth Stevenson and Bryan Spinks (eds), *The Identity of Anglican Worship* (London, 1991), pp. 1–13.

35. *Letters and Papers from Prison. The Enlarged Edition* (London, 1971), p. 300.

2 Michael Ramsey: Catholic Theologian

James E. Griffiss

'Wherever the bishop shows himself, there shall the community be, just as wherever Christ Jesus is, there is the Catholic Church.' So wrote St Ignatius in the earliest Christian use of the Greek word *katholika*.[1] As Kelly goes on to say,

> Here there is no thought of the antithesis between the one orthodox Church and the dissident conventicles. The writer was comparing the universal Church, directed by Christ, with the local churches presided over by the bishops; and his point was that the local community only had reality, life and power in proportion as it formed part of the universal Church with its spiritual head.

Alas, matters have not been so simple since then. The term 'bishop' has undergone changes not only in ordinary usage (many people in the United States, for example, now call themselves 'bishop' whom Ignatius would have difficulty in recognizing), but also in meaning and significance. It has become a disputed term for many Christians – rejected by some and adulated, even idolized, by others. Michael Ramsey considered himself a bishop of the Catholic Church in its local manifestation as the Church of England and in the somewhat broader Church of the Anglican Communion. That is to say, he considered himself to be, and was considered by many others to be, a bishop who presided over a community of the Catholic Church.

© 1995 James E. Griffiss

29

Because he was a bishop of the Catholic Church, he also considered himself to be, and was considered by many others to be, a Catholic theologian, witnessing to and teaching about the same Christ as had Ignatius and living in the same community in which Ignatius himself had lived.

Consequently, the title of this essay, 'Michael Ramsey: Catholic Theologian', must be clarified. We can leave to one side the question of Michael Ramsey as a bishop and whether or not Ignatius would have considered him a bishop. The primary question for this essay is, What does it mean to say that Ramsey, as a theologian, was a witness to and teacher of *Catholic* theology? What is it to be a 'Catholic' in theology?

'Catholic' early on became a more complicated term as the Church faced various schismatic and heretical movements. More and more it came to mean 'orthodox' teaching as opposed to heretical groups or pseudo Churches, such as the rival Churches of Arianism, Donatism, and the like. However, the primary sense in the period when the creeds were developing was still that of the universal Church, teaching orthodox theology, rather than 'the conventicles of heretics'.[2]

However, as any student of the history of doctrine well knows, defining orthodoxy as opposed to heresy and the true Church as opposed to 'conventicles' is fraught with difficulty, and so the term 'Catholic' has had a checkered history, in both East and West. In the West, matters were somewhat simpler (although not by any means simple) as long as the primacy of the Chair of Peter in Rome over all Christians could be maintained. Catholic more and more came to mean what Rome believed and taught, and the growth of papal power provided a way to determine the meaning of the Catholic Church. This relative simplicity was dramatically altered by the Reformation: the Reformers could still claim to be 'Catholic' even while denying the authority of the Roman pontiff and disputing many of the doctrines which Rome taught as orthodox or Catholic.[3]

After the Reformation Rome continued to deal with the problem by asserting its unique claim to Catholicity as both universality in jurisdiction and orthodoxy in teaching. For some time Rome maintained this sense of the word in an exclusive way, so that all who were not in communion with Rome were completely excluded from the 'Catholic Church'.[4] More recently, Rome itself became somewhat more open, as when the Second Vatican Council, in *Lumen gentium*, art. 15, granted that signs of Catholicity could be found in other Christian groups. Even more recently, however, some retreat from that more open position may be evident in the response of the Congregation for the Doctrine of the Faith to the ARCIC Reports, especially in the insistence that doctrinal agreements must be expressed in terms which conform to Roman Catholic usage.[5]

In a dictionary article he once wrote, Michael Ramsey himself said that Anglicanism 'has claimed catholicity through retaining the scriptures, creeds, sacraments and historic episcopate in continuity with the ancient church', but all the while he granted that there is still more controversy about what is to be identified as the Catholic Church.[6]

Certainly, one could argue that the Anglican claim, made there by Ramsey and by many other Anglicans in other places, is not without its own ambiguities. In Anglicanism itself the term is variously used: the terms 'Anglo-Catholic' and 'Catholic Anglican' often imply a party within the Church which emphasizes certain characteristics of Anglicanism (ritual practices, a particular view of orthodoxy, the exclusive claims of apostolic succession, and the like), or the more general way in which Ramsey, following the Chicago–Lambeth Quadrilateral, uses it, that is, arguing for the continuity of Anglicanism with the ancient Church through certain 'signs' of Catholicity.

In his first major writing, *The Gospel and the Catholic*

Church, Ramsey elaborated somewhat upon the meaning of Catholicity for Anglicanism. After pointing out that 'Catholicity' is 'often linked to a piety which is individual-istic and to systems which are sectarian and incomplete', he goes on to say that the 'essence of Catholicism' is to be found 'in the unbreakable life to which the sacraments, scriptures, creeds and ministry have never ceased to bear witness', and that this essence is to be found by searching behind and within for the fact of the *Corpus Christi*, the *soma Christou* in worship and ecumenism but even more in the gospel:

> Catholicism, created by the Gospel, finds its power in terms of the Gospel alone. Neither the massive polity of the Church, nor its devotional life, nor its traditions in order and worship can in themselves ever serve to define Catholicism; for all these things have their meaning in the Gospel, wherein the true definition of Catholicism is found. . . . The claim of Cath-olicism is that it shows to men the whole meaning of the death and resurrection of Jesus.[7]

In effect, in this his first book he established two funda-mental qualifications for Catholicity: first, the Church's 'life', to which the 'notes' of Catholicity bear witness, the Body of Christ as a continuing body of worship and belief; and second, the gospel, the death and resurrection of Christ and the free gift of salvation which that event creates for human beings.

Ramsey wrote *The Gospel and the Catholic Church* in order to appeal beneath or beyond the historic divisions of Catholic and Protestant, especially with regard to the apostolic ministry, to that which unites the two traditions. He was concerned to show that episcopacy should not be a point of division between the two traditions because it was, indeed, at the centre of the Catholicity of the Church which the gospel itself proclaimed. In doing so he made *The Gospel and the Catholic Church* a major Anglican contribution to an ecumenical theology.

I believe the study also set the tone or established the

theme which was to be present consistently in his own work as a Catholic theologian, namely, the necessity of getting behind or beyond external signs and structures to the foundation itself, Jesus Christ, the Incarnation of God.

In order to understand Ramsey's contribution to the tradition of Catholic theology, it is important to see this theme, because, of course, linking Catholicity to the 'life' of the *soma Christou* and the gospel does not resolve the problem of ambiguity. Many Christian communities, indeed probably all of them, would claim that they have continued in the worshipping life of the Church, and they would certainly claim that they are preaching the gospel. Since the Reformation especially, all these theological terms have had as vexed a history as 'Catholicity'. As Christians have discovered after many years of sometimes frustrating ecumenical conversations, appeals to signs of Catholicity (apostolic ministry, creeds, and so on) and even appeals to fundamental Christian beliefs, such as the gospel, do not resolve problems about which there may well be considerable disagreement. As important a contribution as *The Gospel and the Catholic Church* was in its time, the vexed question of apostolic ministry in the episcopate still remains as a barrier for many Christians, and there is still considerable dispute about what may constitute the gospel in the Church. The book, therefore, is important also for what it tells us about Michael Ramsey as a theologian.

Bishop Ramsey's awareness of the continuing disagreement among Christians as to the nature of Catholicism led him more and more to emphasize the fundamentals of Christian faith rather than external signs of polity and practice. In his many conversations with other Churches his emphasis was increasingly upon what he called 'holiness', the desire for God, union with God, our transformation in Christ. The life in Christ, he saw, was what bound Christians together. This fact about Ramsey is delightfully illustrated in an anecdote told about him. On one occasion when as archbishop he was to give a television interview on aspects of Christianity today, he was asked what he would like to talk about. 'Well,' Ramsey replied, 'I should like to talk about God.'[8]

And indeed he always did; God was the subject, no matter what might be the topic of discussion.

I shall, then, want to argue in this article that what makes Ramsey a 'Catholic theologian' is that the subject with which he was always concerned was God – God at the centre of the Church and God at the centre of the life of all human beings; and further that this God at the centre was not just 'God' in general, in the abstract, but God in Jesus Christ, the Incarnate God whose death and resurrection *is* the gospel and whose presence among us is the 'life' of the Church and the world.

In another early article Bishop Ramsey linked his understanding of Anglican theology closely to the doctrine of the Incarnation. After acknowledging the origin in Richard Hooker of the particular Anglican method of theology in scripture, tradition, and reason, he went on to say:

> It was congruous with all this that the Incarnation, with the doctrine of the Two Natures, was central, and that the Church and the Sacraments were closely linked with the Incarnation. The claim of this theology to be 'Catholic' rested not only upon its affinity with antiquity but upon the true 'wholeness' of its authorities and of its treatment of man and his need. It offered him not only justification in his inward self but the sanctification of his whole being through sharing in the divine life.[9]

This is the theme which I shall hope to develop.

With the exception of William Temple, Ramsey wrote more extensively than any archbishop of Canterbury in recent times. Most of his writing was theologically *ad hoc*, in response to particular theological movements as they were developing in the Church, or pastoral, reflecting his involvement with social and political issues. Only three books stand out as sustained theological efforts: *The*

Gospel and the Catholic Church, *The Glory of God and the Transfiguration of Christ*, and *From Gore to Temple*, and none of these is what might be called a 'systematic theology', as that term was used by Stephen Sykes in his criticism of Ramsey and other Anglican theologians.[10]

Consequently, one cannot look in Ramsey's theological writings for a unified structure, a system of belief and practice, nor even a consistent analysis of the dogmatic tradition. Rather, one must look for a unifying image, a central theme, which can unite his extensive writings. That image or theme I would take to be the Incarnation of God in Christ. I say image or theme because for Ramsey, as for many other Anglicans (William Temple, for example), the Incarnation is something more than a doctrine. Certainly it is a doctrine, and as such one which he, along with most Christians, held to about the person and natures of Jesus Christ. But the idea of Incarnation in Ramsey's theology is not just a teaching set alongside other teachings; it rather functions as a governing image, one which interprets everything else in the Christian belief about God and the world. It functions within his theological and pastoral work in much the same way that justification can be said to function in Luther's theology or the Holy Trinity would seem to function in much theology of the Orthodox Churches: that which unites all other doctrines about God and the world and which provides the fundamental interpretation of the human relationship to God. The Incarnation of God in Christ is the centre of that continuing 'life' which Ramsey thought was the essence of the Catholic Church.

However, Incarnation itself is a controversial doctrine, and, therefore, no less a term with an ambiguous history. As far as I am aware, except for a chapter in one book, *God, Christ and the World* (which I shall discuss later), and some occasional essays on New Testament questions, Bishop Ramsey never wrote explicitly on what he thought the doctrine of the Incarnation meant. Rather, he wrote about what it meant to other people, especially to those

35

with whom he shared a common tradition: the Lux Mundi group and Liberal Catholicism which continued the work of Lux Mundi and F. D. Maurice. From those writings it is possible to discern what he saw as the strengths and the dangers of making the doctrine of the Incarnation the centre of theological reflection – dangers which he himself tried to avoid, and strengths which he developed.

The traditional statement of the doctrine of the Incarnation is the Chalcedonian Definition. The Council of Chalcedon was concerned to mediate between conflicting views of the relationship of humanity and divinity as they had arisen in the Church since the creed formulated by the Councils of Nicea and Constantinople, although its definition also led to other controversies. Basically, however, and this is certainly what it meant to Ramsey's theological tradition, the Definition of Chalcedon asserted belief in the full humanity and full divinity of Jesus Christ, that neither nature might, so to speak, overwhelm or negate the other, but that they together form a unity in what Chalcedon called the one Person or Hypostasis of the Incarnate One, Jesus Christ.

For Hooker, to whom Ramsey had appealed in his article, 'What is Anglican Theology?', and to the group which produced Lux Mundi and Liberal Catholicism, the Chalcedonian Definition had distinct consequences for the doctrine of the Church and the relationship of human beings to God. For Hooker it can be summed up in the word 'participation', that, as a consequence of the Incarnation of God in Christ, our humanity has been taken up into the Divine Life, a life in which we participate now in the sacramental life of the Church.

> Thus therefore we see how the Father is in the Son and the Son in the Father; how They both are in all things, and all things in Them; what communion Christ hath with His Church, and His Church with every member thereof in Him by original derivation, and He personally in Them by way of mystical association wrought through the gift of the Holy Ghost, which They that are His receive from him, and

together with the same what benefit soever the vital force of His Body and Blood may yield, yea by steps and degrees They receive the complete measure of all such divine grace, as doth sanctify and save throughout, till the day of their final exaltation to a state of fellowship in glory, with Him whose partakers they are now in those things that tend to glory.[11]

For the Lux Mundi group it meant, primarily, that human intellectual and scientific development which seemed to challenge biblical authority was not to be met simply by entrenchment behind the multiplication of old dogmas. Rather, a religion of the Incarnation should be able to restate old truths in the light of new developments:

The real development of theology is . . . the process in which the Church, standing firm in her old truths, enters into the apprehension of the new social and intellectual movements of each age . . . and is able to assimilate all new material, to welcome and give its place to all new knowledge, to throw herself into the sanctification of each new social order, bringing forth out of her treasures things new and old, and showing again and again her power of witnessing under changed conditions to the catholic capacity of her faith and life.[12]

F. D. Maurice, whom Ramsey greatly admired and whose writings his series of lectures, *F. D. Maurice and the Conflicts of Modern Theology*, and the last chapter of *The Gospel and the Catholic Church* reintroduced to the British (and American) theological world, was also an important figure in the continuation of the Incarnational tradition in Anglicanism. Maurice, Ramsey maintained, was the source for the unlikely marriage between the Tractarians and that movement which was eventually to produce Liberal Catholicism. What he especially admired in Maurice, and what he saw as his most significant contribution, was Maurice's relating of the doctrine of the Church to the doctrine of humanity as recapitulated in Christ:

He saw the possibility of applying the sacramental principle

37

to the common life no less than to the institutional Church. Hence *The Kingdom of Christ* is a prophetic work. Its method foreshadows the social sacramentalism of Stewart Headlam and Scott Holland, the cosmic conception of the Church taught today by French Roman Catholic theologians and the more Biblical presentation of the Church as the Israel of God.[13]

Writing of the sociological concerns which arose from this 'marriage', Ramsey goes on to say,

The theology of *Lux Mundi* saw the Incarnation and the Church in a cosmic relation, the sociology saw human brotherhood as the corollary of both. Where the theology and the sociology were consciously held together, as in the Christian Social Union, the name of Maurice was revered as a father and a founder.[14]

Bishop Ramsey, however, was not unaware of the problems to which this emphasis upon the Incarnation could lead. In his Hale Lectures, given a few years after his book on Maurice,[15] Ramsey asked the question: 'Is there an inevitable loss in theological perspective or proportion if the Incarnation is allowed to become the centre of theology?' He saw several dangers. First, there was the danger that with the Incarnation at its centre, theology can make too much of *explaining* the world and forgetting the absolute need of the cross in a world which 'cannot be explained until it has been radically changed'. Second, that the dominance of the Logos tradition can mean that revelation can become rationalized:

Such rationalism may appear in a tendency to speak as if we moved progressively from discerning God in nature to discerning Him in man, and thence to discerning Him in Christ – whereas it may be that it is only through knowing God in Christ that we are able to believe in Him in relation to nature and man.[16]

And, finally, that too great an emphasis on Incarnation

38

may result in a neglect of other biblical categories, categories which Incarnation does not include.

However, its strengths are still evident in its enabling a genuine meeting between the ancient faith of a supernatural religion and the crises and questions of a contemporary culture. Even more, however (and this, I believe, is where Ramsey's own incarnationalism is most obvious), 'it [Liberal Catholicism] conserved in modern Anglicanism that sense of the creature's adoration of the Creator which the doctrine of the Word-made-Flesh keeps ever at the heart of religion'.

At the end of *From Gore to Temple* he expanded somewhat upon that evaluation by looking at its consequences for the future work which Anglican theology had yet to do.

> There is, however, a distinctive witness still to be borne by Anglican theology out of the depths of its own tradition. . . . There is here a task that Anglican theology can yet perform, by keeping alive the importance of history in the manner of its great divines of the past, by strenuous attempts to relate Biblical revelation to other categories of thought in the contemporary world, by striving to integrate dogma with spirituality in the life of prayer, by presenting the Church as the effectual sign of the supernatural in the midst of the natural order.[17]

It was indeed to this work that Ramsey set himself as Archbishop of Canterbury: to carry out the theme of an Incarnational theology in the new conditions of the postwar period. In that work the Christian doctrine of creation in its relation to the Incarnation of God in Christ became especially important.

Ramsey attributed his understanding of the theological significance of the doctrine of creation and its relation to redemption to F. D. Maurice, even though he recognized the limitations in Maurice's views.[18] It was Maurice who turned him away from the classical exponent of a Reformation theology of creation, Karl Barth, to one which more reflected an Incarnational understanding of the relation of the world to God. In a letter written later in his life Ramsey remarked:

> I never pursued Barth's Dogmatic Theology but the prophetic teaching in Barth's Commentary on Romans made a deep impression on me, with a kind of theological dark night in which I felt I saw humanism, liberalism, ecclesiasticism and devotional pietism as all being under divine judgement. It was Barth's influence which caused me to write in the sharp way about death and resurrection in the first few and last few pages of *The Gospel*. It was this that caused me to try to see the Church's roots in death and resurrection and also to see more positively the significance of Reformation theology. This influence of Barth was a rapid experience, and I moved away from it fairly soon, learning from Maurice the great importance of the Doctrine of Creation which Barth seemed to me to miss so seriously.[19]

Of course, what he meant by this judgement on Barth is true only of Barth's earliest work, and there is no indication, as far as I can determine, that Bishop Ramsey read much beyond Barth's *Romans*. In addition, it would not be true to say that Barth 'missed' the doctrine of creation, but rather that he had a different approach to it. However, I believe Ramsey's meaning for his own thinking is clear. He saw Barth as standing for a theology of creation which too strongly separated the doctrine of creation from a theology which is centred around the Incarnation, one which, consequently, undervalued many of the theological insights in Anglicanism which he considered important.

It can, I believe, be said that the understanding of the relation of creature to the Creator marks off one style of theology from another. Were it not for the fact that there are too many exceptions to the rule, one could argue that how the relationship is understood and carried out in other areas characterizes the differences between Catholic theology and the theology of the Reformation. Such a characterization would be true only in the most general sense, but there is some sense in which it is a true judgement. Certainly, the main emphasis of Catholic theology has derived from a stronger sense of the mediation of the Divine through human, historical, and even material forms than would be found in much of the theology which emerged from the Reformation. Catholic sacramentality, for example, is more prone to accept a spirituality of participation: the material – water, bread and wine, the human person – as a sign or medium of divine presence, than is the theology of the Reformers, which emphasized the greater gulf between God and the sinful and broken world of the human and natural order. In addition, the Anglican tradition with which Ramsey identified himself placed great emphasis upon the role of reason and history in the development of Christian teaching. Catholic theology and spirituality, as Ramsey understood them, have been characterized, that is, by an understanding of grace, faith, and divine action as fulfilling and completing the natural order, rather than as an intrusion into it. Thus Ramsey wrote in his book on the controversy about 'secular religion', *God, Christ and the World*, that secularized Christianity has been developed by

> thinkers whose theological background is that of a Barthian kind of biblical theology where there is no interest in the sacramental view of the created world as Catholic thought has developed it. Secularized Christianity is often a reaction from a pietism which sees no relation between Christianity and the world's culture and a theology which lacks a positive doctrine of the natural order.[20]

Of course, this tendency in Roman Catholic theology at the time of the Reformation led to many abuses, to which the Reformers quite rightly objected; and it led as well to those limitations in Liberal Catholicism to which Ramsey himself alluded. At its best, however, it resulted in a theological method which has been able to see the coherence between creation and redemption in the Incarnate Christ and so to a method which was able to value historical development in doctrine and the genuine contri-

41

bution of the physical and human sciences to an under-standing of Christian faith. Bishop Ramsey himself discussed this aspect of a Catholic and Incarnational theology in several of his writings after he became Arch-bishop of Canterbury.

In his Holland Lectures in 1964, he argued that a biblical view of the relation of human beings to God is a duality, not a dualism; it is one in which we can see the divine image in created human beings, an image which always calls human beings into friendship and fellowship with God and, at the same time, sees the createdness of human beings as grounding us in the material, physical world with its sin and corruption.[21] Thus he was there concerned to see the redemptive coherence between Creation and New Creation in Christ, the Incarnate One in whom the divine image is fulfilled.

He continued to develop this sense of a duality rather than a dualism in his small book to which I have already referred, *God, Christ and the World*. In the Preface he wrote:

> I set myself in this book to examine some of the contemporary theological trends – the concepts of secular Christianity, the existentialist treatment of Christian doctrine, and some aspects of New Testament study. My conclusion is that while the historic faith of Christianity stands, and it is more than ever necessary to assert its supernatural character, it is only possible to do so convincingly if we are ready to learn much from the contemporary conflicts. In particular, if we are to convey to secularism the belief in transcendence, it must be a transcendence realized in the midst of secular life and not apart from it.[22]

He states what he considers to be the truth of the Christian understanding of transcendence in this way:

> The truth of God's transcendence still stands. God is near, but God is different. God is here, but man is dependent. God's otherness is the otherness of Creator to creature, of Saviour to sinner; and it is for the creature still to worship the Creator

and for the sinner still to ask for the Saviour's grace . . . the transcendent and the numinous are to be seen not in a separated realm of religious practice but in human lives marked by an awe-inspiring self-forgetfulness, compassion, humility and courage.[23]

In this little book Ramsey also discusses a theme which was essential to his understanding of an incarnational theology: Jesus as the Incarnate One. He looks first to the New Testament and the titles and images used there to describe the emerging belief in Jesus as Lord, and he concludes that the climax of this New Testament development is to be found in John's Gospel where the imagery used places Jesus in a cosmic setting.

The divine Word has been at work in the world ceaselessly, in creation, in the processes of nature and history, giving life to mankind and illuminating human minds with truth. Now comes the climax. In Jesus the divine Word is fully and finally revealed. While this final act is the goal of the divine energy at work through nature and history, it is also an act of self-giving by One who is beyond history, the Word, the creator, divine. . . . *That* is what Christianity means by the Incarnation.[24]

In language that is not too far removed from that of the Liberal Catholicism of the past, Ramsey speaks of the Incarnation as the act or event which gives meaning to our humanity and to our sense of God:

Thus it is in Jesus that we see man becoming his true self, in that giving away of self which happens when man is possessed by God. The meaning of what it is to be man appears when man is the place where deity fulfils himself, and the glory of the one is the glory of the other.[25]

It is, I believe, appropriate to end this essay on Michael Ramsey as a Catholic theologian on the note of Glory. The Glory of God was the subject of his early book on the transfiguration, and it was a constant theme throughout all his writing, preaching, and teaching. The inscription on his memorial plaque in Canterbury Cathedral is from St Irenaeus: 'The Glory of God is the living man; And the life of man is the Vision of God'.

The Incarnation, as he understood it, was the event in which God's Glory dwelt with us and enabled us to participate in the Divine Glory. The Glory of God in Jesus is, finally, the life of the Church and the source for the Church's unity and of our vision of God. It is what drove him to move beyond the divisions which have afflicted the Church and to ground its unity not in external signs but in the 'life' of the Catholic Church, the truth and holiness which is the gospel.

The final word of the creature to the Creator is adoration, the acknowledgement of who we are in Christ. This is what the Incarnation meant to him, and so in his last book, *Be Still and Know*, he summed up his deepest sense of what it signifies for the Christian life and for the Catholic Church:

Christian prayer and Christian life are properly inseparable. As the sonship of Jesus on earth was a relation to the Father in words, in wordless converse and in obedience of a life and death, so the adopted sonship of the Christians has its facets of word and silence and act. The Sonship of Jesus was to the Father's glory, and in the serving of that glory he consecrated himself on the world's behalf. So too the Christians know the worship of God to be first of all and know also that this worship is an idolatrous perversion unless it is reflected in compassion towards the world. . . .

Within the worship of the Christians are acts of wonder at the beauty of God in the created world and his transcending holiness beyond it; and acts of gratitude for his costly redemption of mankind in Jesus. It is a worship in which sometimes the mind and the imagination dwell upon God's beauty and goodness, and sometimes mind and imagination enter the darkness as the unimaginable love of God is poured into the soul. It is a worship whereby the pain of the world is held upon the heart in God's presence, and the desires of men are turned towards the desire of God as we pray in the name of Jesus.[26]

Notes

1. J. N. D. Kelly, *Early Christian Creeds* (New York: David McKay, 1972), p. 385, quoting from *Smyrn.* 8, 2.
2. Kelly, p. 386, quoting Ildelfonsus of Toledo, *Lib. de cognit. bapt.* 73.
3. See Calvin, *Institutes*, Bk iv, ch. 1.
4. Some Anglican Catholics, of course, have also excluded other Churches, although for somewhat different reasons. This has been one of the unfortunate consequences of the Tractarian revival. It was one of the factors in the rejection of the scheme of union between the Church of England and the Methodist Church which so distressed Archbishop Ramsey. See his address to the General Synod, in *Canterbury Pilgrim* (London: SPCK, 1974).
5. See Henry Chadwick, 'Anglican Ecclesiology and its Challenges', *Anglican Theological Review*, LXXVI, No. 3.
6. 'Catholicism', in *A New Dictionary of Christian Theology* (London: SCM Press, 1983).
7. *The Gospel and the Catholic Church*, 2nd edition (London: Longmans, Green, 1956). Reprinted by Cowley Publications (Cambridge, Mass.: 1990), pp. 174, 175, and 179–80.
8. David L. Edwards, 'The Gospel and the English Church', in Christopher Martin (ed.), *Great Christian Centuries to Come: Essays in Honour of A. M. Ramsey* (London and Oxford: Mowbray, 1974), p. 45.
9. 'What is Anglican Theology?' in *Theology*, vol. 48, January 1945.
10. Stephen W. Sykes, *The Integrity of Anglicanism* (London and Oxford: Mowbray, 1978).
11. *The Laws of Ecclesiastical Polity*, Bk V, lvi, 13. I have quoted from the Oxford Edition of 1890. This dimension of Hooker also continued in the Oxford Movement and its revival of sacramental theology, although it was often overshadowed by other concerns of that movement. For a further discussion, see my *Church, Ministry and Unity: A Divine Commission* (Oxford: Basil Blackwell, 1983), ch. 2.
12. *Lux Mundi: A series of Studies in the Religion of the Incarnation* (ed. Charles Gore), Preface to the 1st Edition, 1889.
13. *F. D. Maurice and the Conflicts of Modern Theology* (Cambridge: Cambridge University Press, 1951), p. 36.
14. Ibid., p. 109.

15. *From Gore to Temple: The Development of Anglican Theology between Lux Mundi and the Second World War* (London: 1960), p. 27. US title, *An Era in Anglican Theology: From Gore to Temple* (New York: 1960).

16. *From Gore to Temple*, pp. 27–8.

17. Ibid., pp. 29, 169–70.

18. See pp. 21–3 in *F. D. Maurice and the Conflicts of Modern Theology*.

19. From a letter to the Revd James Lemler in reference to his thesis for the Master of Divinity degree, 'Reflections upon Divine Glory: The Life and Theology of Michael Ramsey' (1976). Unpublished manuscript in the Library of Nashotah House, Nashotah, Wisconsin. After his retirement, Bishop Ramsey lectured at Nashotah House regularly for several years.

20. *God, Christ and the World* (London: SCM Press, 1969), p. 43.

21. *Sacred and Secular: A Study in the Otherworldy and This-Worldly Aspects of Christianity* (New York: Harper & Row, 1965). See especially ch. 1.

22. *God, Christ and the World*, p. 7.

23. Ibid., pp. 29–30.

24. Ibid., p. 95.

25. Ibid., p. 100.

26. *Be Still and Know* (London: Faith Press, 1982), p. 120.

3 Michael Ramsey and the Orthodox Tradition

A. M. Allchin

It is a fact which has been too little noticed that in the twentieth century, at least two of the archbishops of Canterbury, Michael Ramsey and Robert Runcie, have been deeply influenced by their contacts with the life and teaching of Eastern Christendom. In the case of Archbishop Runcie this influence came largely through his frequent visits to Greece, the Middle East and Romania. Through his travels he has come to have a remarkable insight into the present situation of the Orthodox Churches and has developed a strong intuitive grasp of their whole position. In the case of Michael Ramsey the contacts tended to be less direct. It is true that as Archbishop of Canterbury he made a number of official visits to the Orthodox Churches, and acted as host at Lambeth and Canterbury to some outstanding Orthodox personalities, among them the Ecumenical Patriarch Athenagoras, and Patriarch Justinian of Romania. But Michael Ramsey was a scholar above all, and it was primarily through books and study that he came to his deep understanding of the theology of the Fathers, and of the Greek Fathers in particular. However, as we shall see, he also had personal contacts with the Orthodox Churches from before his ordination onwards, and no account of his work as a theologian and teacher would be complete which did not recognize the profound influence which Eastern Orthodoxy had on the development of his whole theological position.

It is not perhaps surprising that Michael Ramsey was not a great traveller in the Orthodox world; for the greater part of this century large parts of Orthodox Christendom have lived under Communist pressure and persecution and it has not always been easy to have contact with the Churches there. Indeed, one of the least expected results of the Russian Revolution was to send a large group of Russian Orthodox scholars, theologians, philosophers and Church historians out into Western Europe in the 1920s. It was through the meeting between members of this émigré community, particularly those involved in the work of the Institut St-Serge in Paris, and a representative group of Western Christians, most of them Anglicans, that the Fellowship of St Alban and St Sergius was established in 1927 to promote better understanding and clearer knowledge between the separated Christians of East and West. Michael Ramsey was throughout his life an active supporter of the work of the Fellowship, and in the years before the Second World War he was a regular participant in its annual conferences.

In these early Orthodox contacts one name stands out, not that of a Russian or a Greek, but a fellow Anglican and a fellow student at Cuddesdon, Derwas Chitty. While a student at New College, Oxford, Derwas Chitty had won a scholarship to study in Jerusalem, and while there he was powerfully impressed by Orthodoxy. Indeed, he was so much moved by his contacts with Eastern Christians that he found himself on the point of being received into the Orthodox Church. This step, however, he did not take. Rather, he resolved that his calling was to be, if possible, Orthodox within the Church of England. So during his lifetime, much of which was spent as incumbent of a small parish in Berkshire, Derwas Chitty lived and prayed, studied and taught in the spirit of the Orthodox Church.

Chitty was virtually unknown during these years, except among scholars concerned with the origins of Christian monasticism. His one major book, *The Desert a City*, which is a study of the first centuries of monastic life in Egypt and Palestine, was little enough recognized in his own time. It is only in the last twenty years that it has come to be generally acknowledged on both sides of the Atlantic as an outstanding and pioneering treatment of its topic. To have said in his lifetime that there was something prophetic in the vision of Derwas Chitty would have seemed to the majority of his friends to have been paradoxical in the extreme. He had the reputation not only of studying the fourth and fifth centuries, but also of living in them – certainly, he did not fit very easily into the twentieth century. Looking back after more than twenty years, however, the proportions appear very different. The desert monasteries whose history he studied had appeared to be almost defunct at the time he visited them more than sixty years ago, but the contemplative life has proved to be more resilient than most people expected. In the last generation, in the Coptic Church in Egypt, the monasteries have seen an astonishing revival. Two of the outstanding spokesmen of that revival, the Patriarch Schenoude and Father Matthew the Poor, are known as spiritual teachers far beyond the confines of their own communion.

Chitty's insights were also prophetic nearer to home. As a young man he had visited Bardsey Island, 'the island of the twenty thousand saints' off the north-west tip of Wales. He had perceived it at once as a place of great holiness, one of those places where the past comes very near to us, and where eternity seems to interact with time. He had seen it above all as a place of monastic prayer, one of those spots in the west of Britain where the monastic movement which had come from the Eastern Mediterranean that he knew so well had very quickly made itself strangely at home.[1] At the end of his life he looked forward to the restoration of the hermit life on the island and on the peninsula which faces it, and to the renewal of the island itself as a place of pilgrimage. Surprisingly enough in the years that have followed his death, both these things have come to pass. Few of us in the 1960s could foresee the revival of interest in spirituality which we have witnessed in these last decades, let alone the ever-increasing interest in Celtic spirituality in particular.

I have dwelt on one of the unknown figures of our twentieth-century history, partly because it seems clear that he was one of the very first people to impress on Michael Ramsey the importance of Eastern Orthodoxy, and partly because, although the archbishop's life was anything but unknown, there were large elements of it which remained to some extent hidden. His own deep concern with Eastern Orthodoxy was one such element; it was something the general public found difficult to take seriously. Yet Michael Ramsey too was a man who sought to unite within himself Eastern and Western Christianity, sought to be, in some sense, Orthodox, while remaining in the Church of England. Certainly, during the years of his archiepiscopate there were not a few in the Orthodox Churches who saw him in that light. Furthermore, Michael Ramsey was also a man who was not afraid to espouse unpopular causes. The importance which he never ceased to give to the topics of prayer and spirituality marked him out in the 1960s as a man who did not hesitate to walk alone.

If Derwas Chitty was an important factor in opening the world of Eastern Orthodoxy to Michael Ramsey, the annual conferences of the Fellowship of St Alban and St Sergius provided the setting in which the future archbishop could become familiar with the worship of the Orthodox tradition at first hand, and come to understand something of its theological depth and riches. It was also the context in which he was able to make friends with Orthodox scholars and theologians. Undoubtedly it was his friendship with Fr George Florovsky which was of the greatest significance at this time. The kinship which they discovered at the theological level was to emerge again in a much more public setting in the first assembly of the World Council of Churches at Amsterdam in 1948. On that occasion among the theological giants both Ramsey and Florovsky stood out, second only to Karl Barth himself. Though the influence of Barth is certainly to be seen in parts of *The Gospel and the Catholic Church*, to many in 1948 it seemed that Ramsey stood nearer to the Russian émigré than to the professor from Basel. I have vivid memories of the same impression in 1952 at the Faith and Order Conference at Lund. During a question and answer session for the youth delegates, Michael Ramsey seemed almost delighted to find how he was shocking his predominantly Protestant audience, Lutheran and Calvinist, with the Eastern Orthodox flavour of his remarks.

When we turn to Michael Ramsey's own writings on this subject, perhaps the first which we should consider dates from 1946. It was written at the time when he was Professor of Divinity at Durham University, and is entitled *The Church of England and the Eastern Orthodox Churches: Why Their Unity is Important*. In this pamphlet the author sets out his thesis very clearly:

> I shall not shrink from making some very big claims: namely that our familiar divisions have their root in the original schism between East and West, that in unity with the East there lies a remedy for many of the problems and perplexities of the whole Church, that the Church of England has a special debt and obligation in the matter, and that the present crisis in Church and world summons our thoughts *Eastwards*.[2]

It would be interesting to compare this pamphlet in detail with a pamphlet published by Derwas Chitty the following year entitled *Orthodoxy and the Conversion of England*. In many features of style and approach the two works are very different, yet both men are totally at one in their affirmation that the nature of the Western Christian tradition cannot be understood in Western terms alone. Michael Ramsey put it like this:

> The lopsidedness of Rome in the later Middle Ages led to the lopsidedness of Luther and Calvin, and the lopsidedness of the Church of England in the eighteenth century encour-

51

aged the separation of the Methodists. But before and behind all the familiar tragedies of division there was the initial tragedy of the schism between East and West, a tragedy which meant that thenceforth all Christendom was maimed. East and West sorely needed one another, and ever since they went their separate ways neither has been able to present the wholeness of Christian and Church life.

In such a view the schism of the eleventh century is seen as 'the supreme tragedy, the parent tragedy of many later tragedies of Christian division'.[3]

It is interesting to read these words in the context of the insistence of the present pope that the Church is a body which needs 'to breathe with both its lungs', the Eastern and the Western. It is not perhaps surprising that a pope who comes from Poland, a country lying uncomfortably between Catholic West and Orthodox East, should have this overwhelming sense of the necessity of unity and reconciliation between the Old and the New Rome. Perhaps if we were not so familiar with it, we should be right to be surprised to find the same insistence in a representative of a Church which lies to the West of the old Christian world. For Michael Ramsey is very clear that we must not be content with any merely local unity between Anglicans and the English Free Churches:

> The unity of Christians in this land must be the expression in this land of the One, Holy, Catholic and Apostolic Church in its richness. This richness cannot be realized so long as East and West are separate. The quest for unity at home must go hand in hand with the quest for unity far beyond home.[4]

Here we find the conviction which Michael Ramsey expressed time and again in the last twenty-five years of his life, that the question of unity is one and indivisible. That means on the one hand that there can be no true and final unity which does not include all; it means on the other that any genuine movement towards unity and reconciliation in whatever direction will in the end assist that overall fullness of unity.

In this relatively early statement, Michael Ramsey points to three fundamental points in Eastern Orthodoxy which he feels Western Christians need to rediscover. The first is 'a vivid realization of the centrality of the Resurrection in Christianity'. He goes on to quote some lines from the Easter canon of St John of Damascus sung in the Easter night service in every Orthodox Church. It is interesting that he chooses lines which stress the universal, cosmic significance of the resurrection. 'That Easter brings the dawning of a new world, and that nature shares in it together with mankind – these are convictions with which the heart of Eastern Christianity throbs.'[5] We shall find this emphasis emerges again.

The second point touches on a different understanding of the sacramental principle: 'If in our Western sacramentalism we have thought of Christ coming to us by the presence in the Eucharist, the East dwells far more upon the lifting up of the bread and the wine and the worshippers into the heavenly places with Christ.' Here too the cosmic aspect of the Eucharist is implied. All things are lifted up in the offering of the Eucharistic gifts.

The third point involves not the sense of our human solidarity with the natural order, but the sense of the solidarity which binds together those on either side of the gulf of death in the communion of saints.

If the Western devotion to the saints has sometimes seemed like an individualistic appeal for the aid of heavenly mediators, the Eastern attitude to the saints seems far more the natural corollary of the Church's family life. The saints and the departed, between whom the Orthodox are unwilling to make a rigid division, are one with us in Christ; and the Orthodox pray both *to* them all and *for* them all, summoning them to join with their brethren on earth in giving glory to Christ, whose Body and members are one.[6]

It is interesting to see these three points emerging again

53

A. M. ALLCHIN

in what must be one of Michael Ramsey's most carefully
considered treatments of the subject of the relations
between Anglicanism and Orthodoxy, the lecture which
he delivered in May 1962 before the University of Athens,
entitled 'Constantinople and Canterbury', in the course
of which he spoke of the Orthodox Church as 'the
Church of the Resurrection, the Church of the Communion of Saints'. In the first part of this lecture he made
a brief but at the same time full statement of his understanding of the history of the Church of England from the
beginning until today. 'Created partly by Celtic missionaries from Ireland and Scotland and partly by Latin missionaries from Gaul, it was, together with the rest of the West
in the early centuries, a part no less of the one undivided
Church.' He dwelt for a moment on one of the greatest of
early archbishops of Canterbury, Theodore of Tarsus, a
Byzantine Greek. After a glimpse at the history of the
Western Middle Ages, he came to the Reformation, and to
its assertion of the supremacy of the Holy Scriptures in all
matters of faith. But at once came the question, How are
the Scriptures to be interpreted?

> That is a question from which theology cannot escape. It is
> impossible to interpret them as in a vacuum. It is possible to
> interpret them in the light of the controversy of a particular
> age, or in the light of one particular doctrine such as justifi-
> cation or predestination. But from the early years of the reign
> of Queen Elizabeth, and increasingly in the subsequent reigns,
> we see in the divines of our reformed Church of England an
> insistence upon the study of the ancient Fathers as a guide
> to the understanding of Holy Scripture in the context of the
> ancient Church.

He noted with special pleasure the question asked by the
first Elizabethan Archbishop of Canterbury during the visi-
tation of his Cathedral Church, 'whether there be a library
within this Church, and in the same Augustine's works,
Basil, Gregory Nazianzene, Hierome, Ambrose, Chrysostom'.[7] Perhaps we should not make too much of it, but it

54

is interesting to note that there are an equal number of fathers from Greek East and from Latin West.

So the Church of England, in the first generations after the break with Rome, gradually but surely built up its own theological method, interpreting the scriptures in and through the early tradition. He quoted Francis White, Bishop successively of Carlisle, Norwich, and Ely.

> The Holy Scripture is the fountain and lively spring, containing in all sufficiency and abundance the pure water of life, and whatsoever is necessary to make God's people wise unto salvation. The consentient and unanimous testimony of the true Church of Christ in the primitive ages is *canalis*, a conduit pipe, to derive and convey to succeeding generations the celestial water contained in Holy Scripture.[8]

He commented on the way in which, as the seventeenth century proceeded, the appeal to the fathers was used less and less in a merely polemical way, as a tool against Rome or the Puritans, and more and more as a method which gave shape to the whole Anglican understanding of Christian doctrine. This development he saw as leading in two directions. First,

> They were led away from being preoccupied with the matters which had been the absorbing concern of the Continental Reformers, namely justification and predestination, and became instead influenced by the proportion of the theology of the Fathers for whom the central doctrine was that of the Incarnation of the Word made flesh, the Person of Jesus Christ, God and man. For the Caroline divines, as for the Nicene Age, the Incarnation of the Son of God became the heart and centre of theology.

This is the doctrine of the Incarnation seen in its full redemptive and soteriological intention, a vision in which the mystery of Bethlehem leads on ineluctably to Calvary and to the Empty Tomb. This Michael Ramsey saw as the characteristic theology of the greatest teachers of Anglicanism in the last four centuries. He mentioned by name Richard Hooker, Lancelot Andrewes, Jeremy Taylor,

> William Law and Waterland (different as they were) in the eighteenth century; Pusey, Maurice, and Westcott (different as they were) in the nineteenth; Gore and Temple in the twentieth. In every one of these divines the Incarnation was central, and in every one of them the debt to the Fathers was constant and profound.[9]

The second trend in Anglican theology which he saw as beginning in the early seventeenth century is the strong aspiration towards the reunification of Christendom and especially towards the union of East and West. He quotes Lancelot Andrewes' prayer 'for the Catholic Church, its development and increase; for the Eastern, its deliverance and union; for the Western, its adjustment and peace; for the British, the supply of what is wanting, the strengthening of what remains in it'. He saw this longing for unity as an inward as well as an outward reality, an aspiration towards that reintegration of theology, prayer and life which he so constantly advocated and so remarkably embodied in himself. Through all the vicissitudes of Anglican history he saw the stream of divine grace sustaining the unity and life of the Church.

> Yet varieties of opinion amongst us have never altered the firm and certain fact that the mysterious life of divine grace and the primitive orthodox faith have continued. . . . Deeper than the voices of controversy or the Church's many human defects has been this continuity of life, mystical and sacramental. Is this not itself the essence of 'holy tradition'?[10]

Later in the same lecture he asked

> what is Holy Tradition but the continuous stream of divine life, which is the very life of God Incarnate and of the Holy Spirit within the Church? This divine life is in the Scriptures, the preaching of the Gospel, the Sacraments, the lives of Christians, the fellowship of the Saints. Such is the Holy

Tradition. In our Anglican theology we do not speak of it precisely as you do. But it is there, with us and in us. . . . The Holy Tradition is God Incarnate living and moving in the whole life of Christians.[11]

It is evident that for Michael Ramsey the appeal to the Christian East implied for a Western Christian a clear statement about the necessary fullness and integrity of the Christian tradition, a divine gift, a divine presence, living and moving in the whole life of Christendom. As a Western Christian he 'cannot jump out of his own skin or borrow the spectacles of another'. He knew himself representative of a Church closely linked with Rome on the one side, a Rome just about to know the explosion of new life brought about by the Second Vatican Council, and on the other side with the world of Protestantism, and in particular at that time with Methodism with which the Church of England was then in deep and earnest conversation. He saw the picture in its fullness and its complexity, and he found that the Eastern Orthodox presence in the picture provided a vital clue to its ultimate wholeness and unity.

For him this was emphatically not a matter of the past alone, or of the Church alone taken in isolation from the whole world in which it is placed. It is at the heart of the teaching of the Fathers, and the Greek Fathers in particular, that the work of God in redemption is something which touches creation in its entirety; nothing is left out. 'While we discuss the theology and Church life of Constantinople, Canterbury, and Rome too, there is around us the modern world wherein is terrible rejection of divine truth and indifference to it.' The question of Christian unity cannot be separated from our approach to the world in which we live, an approach which needs to be probing yet confident, knowing that God is already present and at work in his creation.

The divine Logos, working in all the created world, the author of all truth, the inspirer of all knowledge properly so called, is working within the scientific methods of our time. If we

57

shrink from saying this we may be in danger of being false to the teaching of the Fathers. If we do say this, then theologians will be conversing not only with one another in the ecumenical exchange but with every sort of other academic discipline, not least those which seem most modern. The theologian will best teach when he is ready to learn and to receive wherever the Divine Wisdom is the teacher.

This is not only a question of academic learning and the search for truth. God is speaking to us no less clearly through the injustice of our world, where 'there is the distress of nations through poverty and hunger, and the distress of races through the lack of brotherhood between them'. And here he turned to one of his favourite quotations from the Fathers:

> to the prophetic words of St Chrysostom, that it is vain to come to the altar in the Eucharist unless we go out to find the altar which is identical with the poor brother: 'This altar thou mayest see everywhere lying both in lanes and marketplaces, and thou mayest sacrifice upon it every hour. When thou seest a poor brother reflect that thou beholdest an altar.'[12]

In the injustices of the system of apartheid, in the blindness which afflicts the nations of the developed world when confronted with the poverty of so large a part of the southern hemisphere, there too the divine Logos is to be heard speaking, speaking in words of judgement and of warning, as well as of the possibility of forgiveness and hope.

The lecture from which we have been quoting was delivered in April 1962. The decade which was just beginning was to be a tumultuous one for all the Churches, not least for the Church of England. The somewhat complacent Anglicanism which had flourished in the previous decade was shattered for ever. The process was an uncomfortable one for Christians of many kinds, including the Archbishop of Canterbury. Yet in the controversies of that time he felt a new life coming into the Church as it sought to respond more directly and more truthfully to the anguish of the age. 'The Church of England is in good heart,' his predecessor had said. It was for him to point out that the heart of the Church might need to be broken,

> and perhaps the heart of the Archbishop broken with it, just because we are here to represent Christ and Christ's compassion. But if that were to happen it wouldn't mean that we were heading for the world's misery but quite likely pointing the way to the deepest joy.

Some months after the publication of *Honest to God* in 1963 the archbishop gathered together at Lambeth a group of theologians representing different points of view within the Church. At the end, in his summing up, he said with great emphasis:

> I believe some of us will have the vocation to stay in the very centre of the Church, representing its tradition and seeing that that tradition is being expounded in a living and creative way, and that others of us will have the vocation to go right out on to the frontiers of the church, to explore new, unprecedented ways of acting and thinking, taking all kinds of risks; and I believe that it will be vitally important that we continue to keep in touch with one another, to respect one another, to listen to one another, even when we disagree, and perhaps particularly when we disagree. It is in that way that we are most likely to come to a new understanding and a new expression of the meaning of the Gospel for our day.

Taken in the light of the concluding section of the archbishop's lecture in Athens we can see in such advice not just an expression of Anglican pragmatism, of a desire to hold together different tendencies within a single Church. We also see an expression of that Orthodox faith which he had sought to expound to his Greek academic audience. In that context he had asked, Can our theology ignore the scientific culture of our day? and had replied, 'I can think of theologies whose nature it would be to say, "Yes, we can ignore it". But such is not the nature of Greek theology or

59

of Anglican, wherever the Greek spirit has influenced it.'[13] We are to look for the action of the divine Logos in all things; at the heart of the Church, but also in the world around it. In that context too he had asked whether the Church, and the theologian within the Church, could ignore the injustices and agonies of the world around him, whether in the contrast between the different regions of our one divided planet, or in the different social groupings within our one divided kingdom. Again the answer had been, God is present there too, Christ meets you in the most despised, neglected, marginalized members of the human family. For Michael Ramsey, inner and outer, past, present and future, time and eternity, all come together and are at one. For him, as another contributor to this volume has pointed out, there was 'no dichotomy between theology and pastoral care, no dichotomy either between theology and prayer'. He had expressed this unity forcefully in his enthronement sermon in Durham in 1952, in commending the words and example of Bishop Westcott to his congregation: 'he stands as a mirror of the tradition handed down to us, a Christianity marked by a passion for truth, a concern for man's common life, and a hunger for another world'.[14]

The other-worldly dimension of this total picture was never far from his mind and heart. Thus, in speaking to his Athenian audience, he had told them of the gifts of monastic vocation within his Church, 'with monks, nuns, friars, who in poverty, chastity, and obedience, serve God both in activity and, like the monks of Mount Athos, in prayer and contemplation'. Similarly, preaching at a pilgrimage Eucharist on Lindisfarne he recalled the examples of Aidan and Cuthbert, going out among the people of their time, 'going all alone in very lonely, very dangerous places', but always coming back seeking to find God alone in the silence and solitude of the desert places, of Lindisfarne no less than Bardsey. Of Cuthbert he declared, 'Back he comes across the sand to be alone with God, alone against the surging sea and the birds flying around him; alone he lifts up his heart to his Creator, praying for the people of this land and for all the children yet unborn.'[15] It was this inward wholeness of life and vision, in which pastoral concern, passion for truth and longing for heaven were constantly intertwined, which he himself embodied. To those who came to know him his seemed to be a life lived out of an experienced knowledge of the peace which comes from above, a life which transfused something of that peace into the affairs of this world and sought at all times to serve the unity and well-being of the Churches of God.[16]

Notes

1. For Derwas Chitty's relationship with Bardsey, see the essay 'The Solitary Vocation' in A. M. Allchin (ed.), *Solitude and Communion, Papers on the Hermit Life* (Oxford, 1977), pp. 9–13.
2. A. M. Ramsey, *The Church of England and the Eastern Orthodox Churches: Why their unity is important* (London, 1946), p. 3.
3. Ibid., p. 4.
4. Ibid., p. 16.
5. Ibid., p. 6.
6. Ibid., p. 6.
7. A. M. Ramsey, *Canterbury Essays and Addresses* (London, 1964), pp. 61–2.
8. Ibid., p. 62–3.
9. Ibid., p. 63–4.
10. Ibid., p. 65.
11. Ibid., p. 70–71.
12. Ibid., p. 72.
13. Ibid., p. 72.
14. A. M. Ramsey, *Durham Essays and Addresses* (London, 1956), p. 88.
15. Ibid., p. 104.
16. For any full treatment of the subject considered in this essay, it would be important to discuss the significance of the transfiguration in Michael Ramsey's thought. On this, see the last chapter in E. C. Miller's valuable work, *Towards a Fuller Vision: Orthodoxy and the Anglican Experience* (Connecticut, 1984), pp. 117–18, one of the few books

which tries to think theologically of the meaning of the relationship of Anglicanism to Orthodoxy, and which reflects the influence of Michael Ramsey's teaching at Nashotah House in Wisconsin during his retirement years.

4 Michael Ramsey and Ecumenical Theology

Gordon Wakefield

Michael Ramsey died wearing the ring, with its emeralds and diamonds, which Pope Paul VI had given him as they parted at the end of his visit to Rome in March 1966. It was a sign betokening the importance in ecumenism both of gestures and of friendship. Michael Ramsey's ecumenism was in part shaped by his friendships, the rapport, not only with Paul VI, but with the Orthodox Patriarch Athenagoras and the Methodist President Harry Morton, to name but two others. It was also determined by the course of his life and ministry. He admitted that, had he remained at York and not been translated to Canterbury, he might not have had many of the encounters which aided reconciliation and made him conscious that there was that, in traditions other than the High Anglican, through which deep called to deep and unity transcended the divisions of history and geography too.

He was brought up in the Congregationalist home of an austere Cambridge mathematics don, a Fellow of Magdalene. He sat in the family pew at Emmanuel Congregational Church from his childhood, and when he listed his benefactors in a meditation during his ordination retreat the name of Henry Carter, the minister, came first (though this may have been because he was attempting alphabetical order). Carter was a fine preacher who influenced many, not least the theologian J. S. Whale, who became his son-in-law, and Whale's own son John, who turned

Anglican and was a prestigious political and religious journalist. But Ramsey found Emmanuel Church too spartan, too puritanical, cerebral and lacking in mystique, and when he was an undergraduate at Magdalene he began to be drawn to St Giles, across the road from the college. The then Anglo-Catholic regime of early communion, prepared for with meticulous devotion, and High Mass, where no one but the priest communicated and the worshipper's mind was free 'for pondering and adoring', matched and fostered his own burgeoning spirituality. He wrote of 'the sense of mystery and awe, and of another world at once far and near . . . a sense that we were vividly in the presence of the passion of Jesus and also vividly near to heaven to which the passion mysteriously belonged, so as to be brought from the past to the present'.[1]

This radical and decisive change of allegiance did not, as we have seen by the inclusion of Henry Carter among his benefactors, lessen his admiration for theologians of the Reformed tradition, such as P. T. Forsyth, who had been minister of Emmanuel Church before Ramsey's time. He has been said to predate both Karl Barth and the Anglican New Testament scholar E. C. Hoskyns, under whose spell Ramsey came at Cambridge.[2] Forsyth's pilgrimage took him 'from [being] a lover of love to an object of grace'. The act of God in the cross of Christ was central. It was the act of a holy God, and Forsyth placed some words of Bishop Butler as an epigraph to one of his books: 'Morality is of the nature of things.' As to the sacraments, he held 'a mere memorialism to be a more fatal error than the Mass and far less lovely'.[3] The Anglican theologian, Canon J. K. Mozley of St Paul's, was a disciple.

Ramsey's Congregationalism reached a kind of climax when, as Archbishop of Canterbury, he was tumultuously welcomed in the Central Hall, Westminster, on the day (5 October 1972) of the union between the English Congregationalists and the Presbyterian Church of England, henceforth the United Reformed Church. He saw it as possibly some compensation for the failed Anglican–

Methodist Scheme and as a modest harbinger of what might yet happen one day in Britain, but he had no direct part in it except in so far as his very presence at Canterbury brought a vestige of ecumenical hope. He represented still the great 'transformation of consciousness', in Adrian Hastings' phrase, which took place in Britain in the 1950s.[4] It is significant that almost a quarter of a century before that union, in a divided electorate, it was the Methodist Newton Flew and the Presbyterian T. W. Manson who proposed and seconded his appointment to the Regius Professorship of Divinity at Cambridge. Before that, while at Durham, he had widened the Anglican Faculty of Divinity to include all denominations.

What must not be ignored in evaluating Ramsey's ecumenism is his political adherence to the Liberal party. He was prominent in Liberal politics at Cambridge, and Asquith, hearing a witty vote of thanks, prophesied that he would one day be leader of the Liberal party. He was always capable of seeing all sides of a question. He hated imperialism and contended for freedom and justice for the individual. He refused to be imprisoned in ideology. He was always a protagonist of clear thinking. He looked to Liberalism as a healer of wounds and divisions, even if sometimes by surgery.[5] This was not submerged when he became a high churchman, though he was not sympathetic to liberalism in theology, and became very critical of his Liverpool mentor, Charles Raven, who was unhappy with his appointment as his successor in the Regius Chair at Cambridge and could not conceal his relief when, after two brief years, Ramsey was made Bishop of Durham. At a dinner in Corpus Christi College, Cambridge, to celebrate the publication of Hoskyns and Davey's *Crucifixion–Resurrection* in 1981, the then Bishop of Ely, Peter Walker, in an attempt to revive a somewhat flagging conversation, mentioned that he possessed a gilt-edged copy of the Streeter symposium *Foundations* inscribed 'W. Temple to his Mother'. 'That doesn't make it a good book,' retorted Ramsey.

His ecumenical theology was not simply dependent on friendships and encounters. It was not a matter of sentiment, but nor was it pragmatic. From his earliest ministry, he stood for unity in the truth and any rapprochement, any scheme, must pass this test. But his Catholic Christianity of its very essence drew him to unity. Catholicism has always held the vision of the 'one Holy, Catholic and Apostolic Church', of a unity which is not mere camaraderie, much less a federation of communions who preserve their independence and agree to differ, but that of an organic whole, the Body of Christ. It is animated not by expediency, or even mutual goodwill, but by the very life of Christ flowing through its members. Only as Christ possesses and is possessed can there be the unity he wills and for which he prayed. This unity is more than that of Galatians 3:28, 'one human being in Christ', the unity which abolishes some of the most essential distinctions of human life, of culture and gender and rank, and renders them void. It is the unity of John 17, of the Lord's consecration prayer at the end of those farewell discourses on which Michael Ramsey loved to dwell, the unity between the Father and the Son in the mystery of the Godhead, the unity which is the very life of God. And this idea of unity is Catholic in that it conforms to the Vincentian canons, 'what has been believed everywhere, always and by all'. So Ramsey 'disagreed with those theologians who said that you could not take theology out of its cultural context, because great teaching has the power of reaching out beyond the frontiers of culture; and therefore radical changes in presentation or interpretation do not prevent an underlying identity in the faith that is believed and the gospel that is preached'.[6]

Ramsey's earliest and most considerable book was *The Gospel and the Catholic Church*, published in 1936 when he was but 32. It was reissued in 1956 with but light revisions. Adrian Hastings' opinion is that it 'has remained a classic of ecumenical theology ... something of a living synthesis not untying all intellectual knots by any means, but pointing forward to the road that Anglicans, and not only Anglicans, would come increasingly to follow'.[7] At a time when the Church was declining and the victim of indifference and a sense that it was no longer relevant, Ramsey sought to help it to recover its Catholic identity, which rests not on papal government or Greek theology but on a death and an empty tomb. The Church is to be itself, standing on its unique foundations whatever the spirit of the age may say.

The book is clearly influenced by Hoskyns. It begins from crucifixion–resurrection, Hoskyns' understanding of the basis of the theology and ethics of the New Testament, and from the New Testament Church as the community which participates in this, supremely through the Eucharist, the focus of its corporate life. Ramsey finds Heiler's famous antithesis between prophetic and mystical prayer too extreme.[8] The pages in which Ramsey expounds this are among his finest writing and the nerve of his theology. The centre of worship 'will not be the needs and feelings of men but the redeeming acts of God and the eternal truths which these acts reveal'. And 'a Christian congregation assembles not to offer "its own worship" to God, but to join as one small fragment in the one act of Christ in his whole Church in heaven and on earth'. Ramsey welcomes the liturgical movement and the Parish Mass (though he came to have reservations about this as a bishop). They must, however, be 'bound up with the return of the Gospel of God'. Catholic order has its deepest significance 'not in terms of legal validity but in terms of the Body and the Cross'.[10] He will not, however, countenance mutual open, or inter-communion, before unity. The Eucharist is not a means, but the end, which brings us to heaven and the unity of the Father and the Son.

The erstwhile Protestant takes the Reformation seriously. He is anxious to fuse his former heritage with his present. At the end of the chapter in which he seeks to evaluate Luther and the Reformation (admittedly more than a decade before the transforming work of the English

Luther scholars Gordon Rupp and Philip Watson), he movingly confesses: 'Catholicism always stands before the
Church door at Wittenberg to read the truth by which she
is created and by which she is judged: "The true treasure
of the Church is the Holy Gospel of the glory and grace of
God." '[11]

Biblical theology was in the ascendant for another
twenty years after Ramsey's first book, and the Liturgical
Movement was about to revolutionize worship through
revision and an agreed shape of the Eucharist in all
denominations. The Second World War speeded the desire
for union as chaplains of different denominations worked
together and learned to understand each other's traditions,
while realizing also what is so evident in our era that
divisions are often more within than between denominations. *The Gospel and the Catholic Church* helped to
set the agenda for all the discussions and hopes for Church
relations in England until as late as 1980. Even more
influential in this was the pamphlet *Catholicity* of 1947,
the report of a group of Anglican Catholics, convened by
Dom Gregory Dix in response to a request by Archbishop
Geoffrey Fisher that they 'examine the causes of the dead-
lock which occurs in discussion between Catholics and
Protestants and to consider whether any synthesis
between Catholicism and Protestantism is possible'.

They were a brilliant team. They included the poet T. S.
Eliot, fresh from the publication of *The Four Quartets*, as
the one lay member. All had books to their name and
many were destined to yet greater influence in the Church.
They covered all branches of theology, and several, sometimes combining it with specialization in other fields, were
famed teachers of spirituality. Ramsey, then Van Mildert
Professor of Divinity at Durham University, was elected
chairman and his hand can be seen in much of the draft-
ing, though it is fascinating to detect other minds, such as
Charles Smyth's, in the claim (not beyond dispute) that

Protestantism has not really come to terms with the reality

of history as the scene of the continuous presence of Divine life that flows from the Incarnation. Partly through a belief that history is intrinsically sinful, partly through the doctrine of *sola fide*, partly through a distorted idea of 'inwardness' and partly through the identification of Rome with anti-Christ, classical Protestantism was unable to conceive of the Church as a Divine life in the context of an imperfect and sinful society. Hence there is in Protestantism an inherited inability to take the visible Church with due seriousness.[12]

It is fair to point out that the pamphlet also seeks to emphasize the positive truths of Protestantism and examines also the achievements and the weaknesses of both the post-Tridentine Papal Communion and Renaissance Liberalism. It is sincere in seeking a synthesis, as Ramsey had always been. Its foundation is that, from the beginning, 'the right order' is not 'Christ – faithful individuals – the Church'; but 'Christ – the Church – faithful individuals'.[13] It is aware of the place of politics in Church history and of political expediency in forming the Church of England. It sees greater possibilities of synthesis in Anglicanism than anywhere else, though these are largely unrealized. It is acutely conscious of 'the sweeping tide of secularism'. In contrast to much teaching of two decades later, it regards secular influence on the various patterns of Christianity it traces as a 'disintegrating virus'.[14]

It is of an irenical spirit which is very much that of Michael Ramsey. It welcomes movements towards synthesis throughout the denominations.

Protestants are seen endeavouring to regain full contact with the Christian ascetical tradition, in studying the ways of prayer and holding retreats. In Scotland and in France, religious communities have appeared within the reformed churches. In the last few years in this country, certain Protestants of the orthodox type have been turning their attention to natural law. Within the Church of England a drastic theological reconstruction is taking place, and the study of the Bible and of early Christianity is leading to the correction of many familiar presuppositions including those which have been held by our own school of thought. In the Roman

Church, the liturgical movement has led to a sustained effort to recover the insights of the period in which the historic liturgies took shape; and since the liturgy consists mainly of Biblical material, this is leading in turn to a Biblical theology which shows great promise.[15]

The pamphlet deplores the bogus unity which is the mere 'sinking of differences' in jolly fraternity. This too often means a tearing up of roots, and the authors would as much regret the disappearance of the old values of chapel as of church. But the old patterns 'do not suffice, for they do not represent the unity for which our Lord prayed'. This must be reborn. It 'will include something of all the patterns ... in their elements of devotion and conviction, of dogma and discipline' But 'the only motive that can truly unite them is a common conviction about the truth of the Gospel and the Church'. The grounds of unity are not that divisions are wasteful, or differences do not matter, or that 'it will make a better impression if we show a united front'. ' "Sanctify them in the truth. Thy word is truth." The fulfilment of the prayer of our Lord comes by the recovery, within every portion of our sundered Christendom, of the reconciliation of His people in the truth.'[16] That is pure Michael Ramsey.

Catholicity produced a rejoinder in 1950, also presented to the archbishop, in *The Catholicity of Protestantism*, by an equally brilliant team of Methodist and Free Church scholars of whom Dr R Newton Flew was chairman. It quotes the Anglican historian R. W. Dixon as saying that the word 'Protestant' in England up to and including the Caroline divines was understood to include the designation of 'Catholic'.[17] It defines Catholic in the terms of Ignatius of Antioch, apparently the first to use it: 'wherever Jesus Christ is, there is the Catholic Church'. 'It is the presence of Christ, recognized, adored and obeyed, which secures the catholicity of the Church'.[18] 'There is no communion on earth which is *fully* catholic, for no communion on earth possesses in the full and absolute sense, the "wholeness" of the Gospel.' This is eschatological and fully realized only in the world to come, and the report challenges the apparent belief of *Catholicity* that there was a time in the first or second century of primitive wholeness when the Church revealed this eschatological perfection. It quotes the Declaratory Statement, drawn up in 1917 and the basis of the Free Church Federal Council of 1941, which no Catholic could fault as embodying the wholeness of the Christian faith. It goes on, with the benefit of the Luther scholarship which Wesley House, Cambridge, had done much to promote through its Finch Travelling Scholarships, to correct *Catholicity*'s misrepresentations of Reformed Theology. It shares *Catholicity*'s hope of a synthesis through unity in the truth of the gospel. It cannot 'reconcile the view that the episcopate is "the essential channel through which sacramental grace flows out into the Church" with the view that it is not essential'. Nor can it contemplate the reordination of Free Church ministers. It thinks it unreasonable for 'Catholics' to lay down conditions of episcopacy to the Free Churches, which are not accepted in the Church of England as a whole, to ask more of them than their own communion demands of its members. But the authors believe that understanding may be reached on many of the subjects hitherto divisive and welcome the unity achieved in South India and conversations taking place in various parts of the world.

The Catholicity of Protestantism is, in some ways, more 'triumphalist' than *Catholicity*. The authors are under the spell of K. S. Latourette's *History of the Expansion of Christianity* and of post-war optimism as to Protestant Christianity's evangelistic future. The World Council of Churches had been founded at Amsterdam in 1948, where Ramsey, elevated into being 'a mouthpiece of the western Catholic tradition', impressed his fellow-consultant Karl Barth, who described him as 'a man with whom I more often agreed than disagreed – *the* outstanding figure in the picture of my first ecumenical experience'.[19] It was an incomplete Council, inevitably coloured by the German

Protestants who had resisted Hitler, with Rome absent in cold hostility and the Orthodox represented by émigrés. Ramsey found another kindred spirit in the Russian refugee George Florovsky, who was one with Ramsey and Barth in refusing to countenance a mere federation as the Church united in the truth.

Until his retirement, Ramsey was faithful to the World Council assemblies, though never totally at home and nervous when the spotlight was on him. He approved the entry of the Greek and Russian Orthodox Churches and the rapprochement with Rome, but was unhappy about the decision of its committee in 1971 to give grants to South African and Rhodesian guerrillas, which some Church of England dignitaries supported. It is tempting to speculate what he would have made of Canberra in 1992 with its tensions between Far Eastern syncretism and Orthodoxy.

Ramsey was well aware that the ecumenical situation was changing, in some sense, as Adrian Hastings said, being transformed, in the course of his episcopates. He was able not only to accept the Anglican–Methodist Scheme of Unity, which went far beyond anything Archbishop Fisher, or even *The Catholicity of Protestantism*, had envisaged, but to lay his archiepiscopate on the line for it. The controversial Service of Reconciliation of ministries, work of two Anglo-Catholics, aimed to avoid the submission of Methodists to reordination while satisfying Catholics that all received a wider commission. The proposed new ordinal won the highest praise.

By failing to reach a sufficient majority for acceptance, Ramsey felt that the Church of England had betrayed its Catholicity, for he had never believed that unity was simply a matter of Anglicans and Rome. The Second Vatican Council was as important for him as for everyone else, and with Paul VI he founded the Anglican–Roman Catholic International Commission (ARCIC), which has produced some remarkable documents, unfortunately not all endorsed by controlling elements in the curia. It is sad that the Council probably contributed to the failure of the

'Anglican–Methodist Scheme by reviving Anglo-Catholic hopes that their dream of union with Rome might soon come true. Some felt that to achieve this they must abandon the Methodists. They were wrong, forgetting *inter alia* how much Romans and Methodists have in common in spirituality, centralization and not being established churches in Britain. They also underestimated Vatican intransigence. In addition, the Anglican ordination of women as priests has not for the time being made fulfilment easier, though one will not forget the applause which greeted former Archbishops Ramsey and Coggan as they followed the procession of John-Paul II and Archbishop Runcie out of Canterbury Cathedral in May 1982. It was mostly for Ramsey, forgiven by those who had thought him misguided in his support for the now forgotten Anglican–Methodist Scheme.

The Gospel and the Catholic Church was not, of course, unopposed in 1936 and certainly is not now. In a discussion at the Queen's College at Birmingham in the mid-1980s, Lesslie Newbigin spoke warmly of it as seminal, while Peter Stephens disagreed from the standpoint of a theologian of the Reformation, reviving the arguments of *The Catholicity of Protestantism*. More recently, an Anglican friend of mine, much influenced by the late Sir Karl Popper, reread it and found it totally unconvincing, cocooned in a world of biblical theology and outdated certainties. Nothing reverberated for him, though he is an admirer of Ramsey. Modern academic theology often lacks the confidence of the 1930s, 40s and 50s. No longer do biblical scholars talk easily of 'assured results'. It is admitted that little is known for sure about the early Church, that the New Testament itself does not give us information either about a unified, uniform organization, or a unified theology. The confidence of the pamphlet *Catholicity* about 'the primitive unity' seems breathtaking. The 'apostolic ministry' is not for certain that of bishops and Church leaders, more of missionaries.[20]

Apostolic succession is more a mystical idea in the mind

of traditionalist theologians than a historical reality to
which a united Church must conform, though many would
now agree that a constitutional episcopacy would be the
only possible organization. Post-modernism destroys old
certainties, while allowing a 'reader-response', which
ignores the author's intentions and original meanings and
is congenial to conservative evangelicals who are so suspicious of the historical criticism which Ramsey, like Hoskyns, regarded as a necessary tool of exegesis. His
penultimate book, *Jesus and the Living Past*, is as convinced as his earlier writings about the theology of Alan
Richardson, that disengagement from history is destructive
error. In this work, he insists against the American, John
Knox, that Jesus is prior to the Church. The Church
existed in utter dependence upon Jesus. 'We need not
hesitate to say that the event of Jesus is distinguishable
from the event of the Church.'[21] This is no modification of
the statement of *Catholicity* that the right order is 'Christ
– the Church – faithful individuals' yet it does not allow
the second term to overshadow the first. It affirms a Jesus
of history about whom we may know a basic minimum
as certain fact. Other historical certainties may not be
necessary. In the words of Herbert Butterfield, important
to John Robinson in *Honest to God*, 'Hold to Christ and
for the rest be totally uncommitted.'

The Bible has lost authority for some because it has its
unedifying passages, from which allegory does not rescue
it as once it did. Furthermore, the New Testament represents the victory of certain views which became orthodox,
sometimes by the suppression of alternatives, and always
because the Church was male-dominated. The Bible itself
comes from a patriarchal society, and the place of women
in the ministry of Jesus and afterwards has been dimin-
ished by sexism. Even Jesus himself called God Father,
never Mother, and some feel that the faith of the future in
an age of women's equality, if not rule, must be post-
Christian. There is a criticism of the records not because
they contain different and perhaps conflicting versions of

events or because their veracity cannot be established by objective history, but because they presuppose the submission of women. They were spectators of Calvary, if not at the foot of the cross as in John, they were first at the tomb on Easter morning, but they were not Jesus' companions up the mount of transfiguration or in the Garden of Gethsemane, and only John and, very briefly, Matthew allow Resurrection appearances to them.

The idea of the Church which inspired Ramsey and the ecumenical movement most of his time has faded. R. Newton Flew's book *Jesus and His Church* which held sway, though not unchallenged, for two or three decades from 1938 and endeavoured to prove that Jesus did found a community, has long passed into the mists of uncertain and conflicting theories. Discipleship may now be seen as the fundamental concept of ecclesiology more than the 'people of God' or 'the Body of Christ'.[22] The Church in history has too often been the creation of Caesaro-Papalism rather than of the Man of Nazareth. In A. N. Whitehead's moving phrase, 'the brief Galilean vision of humility flickered' and almost died.[23] Constantine has been seen as a semi-pagan disaster, his 'establishment' of Christianity its perversion. We cannot escape Dostoevsky's story of 'The Grand Inquisitor'.

The Catholics in the Church of England have declined, torn apart by their own divisions over unity with the Free Churches and, even more seriously, over women's priesthood. Some have gone to Rome and others are on the way, while the rest seem divided between the reactionary Forward in Faith and the greater liberality of Affirming Catholicism. There is also the non-realist Sea of Faith movement. But the greatest increase is in evangelicalism. For more than a quarter of a century, evangelicals have taken to Catholic liturgy, their bishops wearing vestments and mitres, their priests deserting the Book of Common Prayer for the Alternative Service Book, but in some places there is almost a flood-tide of corybantic worship and charismatic enthusiasm. Ramsey hoped that liturgy might be, after centuries of bitter controversy, a focus of unity. In 1963 he took the initiative in the formation of the Joint Liturgical Group, which still exists for the service of the British Churches, now including the Roman Catholics, to study questions of liturgy in general, investigate principles of Christian worship, and provide common orders when desired. Some Free Churchmen have become immensely learned in the subject, and the Eucharist is recognized as central in many of the mainstream denominations. There is a feeling, however, that liturgy does not now sufficiently express the new enthusiasm, and there is demand for informal worship, lively and loud, guided by the immediacy of the Spirit. There is less revival of in-depth evangelical theology with its roots in classical Calvinism, which tends to deplore the charismatic, than of a very personal pietism typified by the slogan 'Smile, Jesus loves you'. Unity is not seen at all in terms of the One, Holy, Catholic and Apostolic Church, sanctified in truth, making present on earth the saving crucifixion–resurrection of Christ, entering in each Eucharist into the Kingdom of God, but of born-again Christians, irrespective of churchmanship. It is a unity of experience rather than of objective and Catholic truth and often measured in terms of calculable 'success', productivity in a world of market forces.

Where there is some vision of Christian community is in the belief that Christians must act together in Christian Aid of the poor, the hungry, the refugees and the victims of injustice. This often means for some anti-racism and feminism. The Parable of the Sheep and the Goats of Matthew 25:31–46, more widely interpreted than in its origin, where the least of Christ's brothers are poor and persecuted disciples, has become a charter of action.

In *The Gospel and the Catholic Church* Ramsey eschews the politicizing of the Church. It is not an institution for social action or moral judgements on social issues. It exists to preach Christ and his death and much which is unintelligible to the world and yet will save it. This was very much the mood of High Church thinkers of the time, like the Methodist T. S. Gregory who became a Roman Catholic layman, editor of the *Dublin Review* and, after the war, in charge of religious broadcasts for the BBC Third Programme. He had written in his Methodist days, ten years before Ramsey's first book, a manual on the sixth beatitude in which he had stated something which helped to make him a Roman Catholic: 'For it is not man's final purpose to cure pain, to throw a cloak of decency over politics and trade, to run churches, orphanages, schools or reformations – but to see God.' At this stage, Ramsey could well have agreed. But as an archbishop, he became aware that the secular world in its needs could not be ignored. He would confront Vorster in Pretoria and intervene with almost irresponsible boldness in a British Council of Churches debate on Rhodesia. In his Scott Holland lectures, 'Sacred and Secular', he takes seriously the radical insistence on this worldly holiness: 'Two worlds are ours.' There is a moving passage towards the end of the book in which, returning to St John, he shows that the Lord's going to the Father is also a journey 'deeper and deeper into humanity with its sin, its sorrow and its death. . . . Towards heaven, towards the world's darkness: these were two facets of the one journey, the one Christ.'[24] In his last book, *Be Still and Know*, he writes similarly:

> The prayer with beautiful buildings and lovely music must be a prayer which also speaks from the places where men and women work, or lack work, and are sad and hungry, suffer and die. To be near to the love of God is to be near, as Jesus showed, to the darkness of the world. That is the place of prayer.[25]

These sentiments would unite many Christians.

The key to Ramsey's ecumenism and his enduring contribution amid so many changes is in his spirituality. This must have been implicit throughout. He once said that the book he was most glad to have written was that on the transfiguration, the second part of his 1949 study, *The*

Glory of God and the Transfiguration of Christ. He traces the treatment of the story in the New Testament, the Fathers and throughout Church history. There is richness here and much to bring those who meditate on it into the divine glory. Ramsey finds in the transfiguration a gospel for the now nuclear times, though it does not belong to the central core of the first proclamation:

> It stands as a gateway to the saving events of the Gospel, and as a mirror in which the Christian mystery may be seen in its unity. Here we perceive that the living and the dead are one in Christ, that the old covenant and the new are inseparable, that the Cross and the glory are of one, that the age to come is already here, that our human nature has a destiny of glory, that in Christ the final word is uttered and in Him alone the Father is well pleased. Here the diverse elements in the theology of the New Testament meet.[26]

The Christian faith must be presented

> not as a panacea of progress, nor as an other-worldly solution unrelated to history, but as a Gospel of Transfiguration. Such a Gospel both transcends the world and speaks to the immediate here-and-now.... No part of created things and no moment of created time lies outside the power of the Spirit, who is Lord, to change from glory to glory.[27]

This book reveals the lure of Eastern Orthodoxy, with its liturgical centrality and its 'outlook more mystical than moral'. He would also agree with Vladimir Lossky in *The Mystical Theology of the Eastern Church*, then only in French, that 'the West shows its fidelity to Christ in the solitude and abandonment of the night of Gethsemane, [the East] gains certainty of union with God in the light of the Transfiguration'. The West, says Ramsey, may miss 'The cosmic context in which the Christian life is set.' The East 'has instinctively honoured the Transfiguration with a special warmth and tenacity' and, free of moralism and the desire always to learn practical lessons, 'has often been content simply to rejoice in the glory which Mount Tabor sheds upon Christ, the Christian and all creation'.[28] Ramsey once expressed to me reservations about Kenneth Kirk's *The Vision of God* (1931) because it confined itself to Western spirituality.

Ramsey could not have contemplated a complete union which excluded the Orthodox. Rome alone, even with other Western denominations, would not have satisfied him. It was surely he who included in *Catholicity* the quotation from Lancelot Andrewes' *Preces Privatae* when he prays

For the whole Church
                    Eastern
                    Western
                    our own

and went on to observe 'a recurring recognition that the Fullness of Tradition is not to be found either in the West or in the East in separation.[29] While he was a teacher at Lincoln Theological College he joined the Fellowship of St Alban and St Sergius, 'an unofficial body which exists to promote understanding between Eastern and Western Christians'.

For Ramsey the way to unity became increasingly through an awareness of this world in its need, but also of a world beyond, of the heaven of Divine glory, where Christ presents his Passion before the eternal altar.

What is called the intercession of Jesus means his ceaseless presence with the Father. He is with the Father, not begging the Father to be gracious, for from the Father graciousness ever flows. He is with the Father as one who died for us on Calvary, with the Father in the presence of a life which is ever, the life that died; with the Father as one who was tempted as we are and bore our sins and our sufferings; with the Father as the focus of our hopes and desires. To approach the Father through Jesus Christ the intercessor is to approach in awareness of the cost of our redemption by a sacrifice made once for all and a victory once accomplished, a sacrifice and a victory which are both past history and ever

present realities. It is this which both enables and character-
ises our response to God through Jesus Christ.[30]

Be Still and Know, short like so many of Ramsey's books,
is yet as comprehensive a study of prayer as could be
wished. No aspect or tradition of prayer is left out, beginning with the Prayer of Jesus himself. Ramsey recom-
mends the Methodist Raymond George's *Communion with
God in the New Testament*,[31] in some ways a rejoinder to
Kirk's *The Vision of God* with an emphasis on prophetic
prayer, though one feels that for him, contemplation is the
heart of the matter. Its passivity 'is a judgement upon
salvation by works' and a manifestation of 'faith alone and
grace alone', and, like Rowan Williams, he sees the link
between the experience of Luther and that of St John of
the Cross.[32] There is unity in prayer, Catholic, Protestant,
Orthodox.

Michael Ramsey's ecumenical theology does not speak
in the strident tones of much contemporary Christianity,
but it has its heirs. It could still be, if Anglicanism remains
faithful to it, the most powerful instrument of the unity of
the whole people of God.

Notes

1. Owen Chadwick, *Michael Ramsey: A Life* (Oxford: Clarendon Press, 1990) p. 22.
2. See Ramsey's Foreword to E. C. Hoskyns and Noel Davey,
   Crucifixion–Resurrection, ed. Gordon S. Wakefield,
   (London: SPCK, 1981); Gordon S. Wakefield, 'Michael
   Ramsey: A Theological Appraisal', *Theology*, November
   1988; and Owen Chadwick, op. cit. pp. 27ff., 45, 49f.
3. *The Church and the Sacraments*, 2nd edition
   (Independent Press, 1947), p. xvi.
4. Adrian Hastings, *A History of English Christianity,
   1920–1985* (Glasgow: Collins, 1986), p. 472.
5. Chadwick, op. cit., pp. 17ff.
6. Chadwick, op. cit., pp. 411ff.
7. Hastings, op. cit., p. 261.

8. F. Heiler, *Prayer* (English translation, Oxford: Oxford University Press, 1932), passim.

9. *The Gospel and the Catholic Church*, (London: Longmans, 1936), p. 94.

10. Ibid., p. 179.

11. Op. cit., p. 180. This paragraph includes some sentences from my article 'Michael Ramsey: A Theological Appraisal' *Theology*, November 1988.

12. *Catholicity* (Dacre Press, 1947) p. 43.

13. Op. cit., p. 13.

14. Ibid., p. 46.

15. Ibid., p. 47.

16. Ibid., pp. 46f.

17. *The Catholicity of Protestantism* (Lutterworth Press, 1950), p. 16.

18. Ibid., p. 21.

19. Chadwick, op. cit., pp. 66f.

20. James Tunstead Burtchaell, *From Synagogue to Church* (Cambridge: Cambridge University Press, 1992).

21. *Jesus and the Living Past* (Oxford: Oxford University Press, 1980) pp. 4f.

22. See Robert Murray in Peter Brooks (ed.), *Christian Spirituality* (London: SCM Press, 1975) p. 69.

23. See Donald MacKinnon, *The Stripping of the Altars* (London: Collins Fontana, 1969, p. 57.

24. *Sacred and Secular* (London: Longmans, 1965) p. 76.

25. Op. cit., (Collins Fount, 1981), pp. 13f.

26. Op. cit., (Longmans, 1949), p. 144.

27. Ibid., p. 147.

28. V. Lossky, *The Mystical Theology of the Eastern Church* (James Clarke, 1957), p. 227; Ramsey, op. cit., p. 135.

29. Op. cit., p. 50.

30. *Be Still and Know*. p. 54.

31. Epworth Press, 1953.

32. *Be Still and Know*, p. 91.

5 Michael Ramsey and Biblical Theology[1]

John M. Court

Biblical theology, in the technical sense, is a movement whose time has come and gone, although an imminent revival (under modified conditions)[2] remains a distinct possibility. However, the insights of biblical theology were the presuppositions with which Michael Ramsey worked in his major writings, so it is appropriate first to define these terms of operation, and then to describe and evaluate the use which he made of them.

The first recorded use of the expression 'biblical theology' is found in 1629, where it is concerned with the 'relationship of theology to its biblical bases'. Beyond this general concern, the highly technical sense of the term, with its implications of a movement directed to this end, belongs in the context of modern biblical scholarship. The effect of such scholarship has been to cause a radical shift from the *prescriptive* sense of the words ('theology that does and should accord with the Bible') to the *descriptive* meaning ('theology contained in the Bible'), though both emphases must still imply that some claim is made on the other sense. As on the banner of a movement, the slogan 'biblical theology' can be used as a religious 'protest against the abstractions and compromises of academic theology'.[3] Such a watchword seeks to remind the intellectual discipline of its essentially religious origins, though it may share the problems experienced by other modern movements

which have used slogans such as 'The Quest of the Historical Jesus' or 'Religionless Christianity'.

Karl Barth's famous commentary on *The Epistle to the
Romans* (1919), translated into English by Edwyn Hoskyns
(1933), can be taken as a powerful symbol of biblical
theology, as of a new orthodoxy. Barth wrote in a preaching
style, not only for directness of communication, but also
for a theological reason. He claimed that the true subject
of the Bible is the living God who confronts humanity
today through the pages of Scripture.

> The historical–critical method of Biblical investigation has its
> rightful place; it is concerned with the preparation of the
> intelligence – and this can never be superfluous. But were I
> driven to choose between it and the venerable doctrine of
> Inspiration I should without hesitation adopt the latter, which
> has a broader, deeper, more important justification. The doc-
> trine of Inspiration is concerned with the labour of appre-
> hending, without which no techical equipment, however
> complete, is of any use. . . . My whole energy of interpretation
> has been expended in an endeavour to see through and
> beyond history into the Spirit of the Bible, which is the Eter-
> nal Spirit.[4]

In any survey of twentieth-century Protestant theology
this commentary is now seen as the cornerstone of neo-
orthodoxy, a conscious replacement and suppression of
'cultural Protestantism' (the liberal interpretation of the
Bible and society, represented by such as A. Ritschl,
W. Hermann and A. von Harnack). But it also represents
a new biblical theology, determined to relate the new
orthodoxy to the Christian study of the Bible. It is no
accident that Michael Ramsey himself quotes from Barth's
commentary in *The Gospel and the Catholic Church* (see,
for example, pp. 40f, 49). Barth had given to the term
'biblical theology', an emphasis on the theological unity of
the Bible (which more recent scholarship finds impossible
to maintain). The pervasive element of biblicism in his
work had a powerful influence against the background of

the rise of Fascism (though it has been seen more critically since). A special enthusiasm for Covenant theology, related to Barth's respect for the work of Calvin, was widely exploited for the next forty years. But, as Robert Morgan observes of biblical theology, 'in academic circles, this ephemeral movement was by 1960 in a state of terminal decline'.[5]

The influence of Karl Barth and biblical theology in Scotland, and especially in America, was vastly more substantial than it was in England.

> Biblical theologians such as L. S. Thornton and A. G. Herbert, and later A. M. Ramsey and A. Richardson, were doctrinal theologians rather than biblical scholars. . . . Anglican writers found a theology of the people of God in the whole Bible, and their revival of the distinctively Christian symbols in an ecclesial environment replaced the worn-out philosophical theology of the 1920s.[6]

For purposes of comparison, the extent of the movement in North America in the 1940s and 1950s can be seen in the account given by Brevard Childs.[7]

However, before all English involvement in biblical theology, including our subject's, is minimalized, it is necessary to examine the evidence by looking at Ramsey's published work and analysing the influences upon him. I believe we shall find a complex thinker, subject to multiple influences and engaging directly and sensitively with the fluctuating contemporary fashions in theology.

In June 1927 Michael Ramsey took a first class degree in theology after four terms' work. He had come up to Magdalene College, Cambridge, in 1923 to read classics. His Part One result was undistinguished, and he decided to read law, for career reasons, then changed again to theology because of his growing sense of vocation. The study of theology brought Ramsey the Anglo-Catholic undergraduate within the influence of Edwyn Clement Hoskyns, the Anglo-Catholic dean of Corpus Christi College. Hoskyns, like Karl Barth, was a converted liberal; the experience of German theology, and especially the reading (and ultimately the translating) of Karl Barth's work, had a formative influence on Hoskyns' lecturing as early as 1923.

In turn, Ramsey was inspired by Hoskyns:

> Hoskyns communicated enthusiasm. He infected his hearers with the sense that this search after religious truth was of urgent importance to humanity. He introduced Ramsey to modern German thought. He showed him the work of Karl Barth. . . . Ramsey always remained critical of Hoskyns. The Christian mind which he revered was then and ever after the mind of William Temple. . . . Ramsey never doubted that in the formation of his mind Hoskyns was influential, and ever afterwards he was grateful. 'I learned from him, more vividly than from anyone else, that the study of the New Testament is an exciting adventure, and that while it calls for a rigorous-critical discipline, it is not made less scientific if the student brings to it his own experience of faith.'

Owen Chadwick concludes that one of 'the basic ingredients of Michael Ramsey's mind' was 'an openness . . . to the European religious reaction against liberal Protestantism, represented especially by Karl Barth'.[8]

Gordon Wakefield identifies 'four characteristics of Ramsey's theology which are clearly due to Hoskyns' influence':

> First, the continuity between the Jesus of history and the Christ of catholic faith . . .
> Second, Christian theology begins from the crucifixion–resurrection of Jesus . . .
> Third, the gospel precedes the Church . . .
> Fourth, theology and history are partners.[9]

Wakefield proceeds to divide Ramsey's theological life into three periods:

> The first and longest is from the publication of *The Gospel and the Catholic Church* to his translation to Canterbury in 1961. This was the time when biblical theology was in the ascendant, and Ramsey grounded his theology in the Bible,

85

studied critically and semantically, in the belief that it was a
unity, the book of the mighty acts of God revealed in
Christ . . .

The second period is that of Ramsey's primacy . . .

The third period is that of Ramsey's exemplary retirement.
He summarized the presuppositions of his theology as he
looked back over his long life.[10]

This is a natural division, although it cuts across the
other natural boundary, between academic and ecclesiastical careers. It serves to emphasize the substantial period,
between the 1930s and the early 1960s, when the themes
and methods of biblical theology, learnt from Hoskyns and
ultimately derived from Barth, dominated Ramsey's
approach to theology. But it is potentially misleading if it
suggests that the underlying theological principles were
radically different in phases two and three. The distinction
is more an external one, recognizing and reflecting,
especially during phase two, the decline of the biblical
theology movement and the new radicalism of works like
John Robinson's *Honest to God*. Ramsey paid them serious
attention, but his heart did not change.

It is time to consider a selection of Ramsey's own writings. *The Gospel and the Catholic Church*, first published
by Longmans in 1936, and lightly revised for a second
edition in 1956, is widely regarded as Ramsey's most
enduring work, and should probably be reckoned as his
best book in terms of its biblical exegesis. Ramsey stated
his intention as 'expounding the Church as a part of the
Gospel of Christ crucified'. He unpacks the meaning in
the following words of the Preface:

The study of the New Testament points to the Death and
Resurrection of the Messiah as the central theme of the Gospels and Epistles, and shows that these events were intelligible
only to those who shared in them by a more than metaphor-
ical dying and rising again with Christ. It is the contention of
this book that in this dying and rising again the very meaning
of the Church is found, and that the Church's outward order
expresses its inward meaning by representing the dependence

of the members upon the one Body, wherein they die to self. The doctrine of the Church is thus found to be included within the Christian's knowledge of Christ crucified.[11]

To James E. Griffiss, in his evaluation of the book fifty years on (in 1986), this 'shows Bishop Ramsey's concern . . . to relate biblical . . . themes to the contemporary concerns of the church', in his earlier, just as in his later, theological writings.

In this book his primary emphasis is upon the cross and its significance for the doctrine of the church, evidently under the influence of Karl Barth. . . . In the first four chapters he provides us with a biblical study of the significance of the cross and resurrection for a theology of the church as the Body of Christ into which the believer is incorporated through the death of Christ, and by doing so he is able to provide a foundation for his subsequent discussions of the meaning of unity, the relationship of the gospel to apostolic order in the episcopate, and the signficance of worship and liturgy for expressing and fulfilling the corporate life of the Body.[12]

Michael Ramsey saw a great opportunity for 'Anglican Catholics', including himself, 'to teach the richest and deepest meaning of the word Catholic and to find the *essence* of Catholicism not in particular systems of government or thought or devotion (Anglican or Latin) but in the organic corporate idea of the Body [Corpus Christi] in life and worship'.[13] In Griffiss's words, Ramsey offered 'a theology of church and ministry that sought to show the deep relationship between the gospel and the life of the church in its several forms of ministry rather than in superficial concerns with validity of orders'.[14]

Of course, it is possible to disagree profoundly with what Ramsey is saying, and the way he uses biblical and historical evidence. Griffiss regards as 'finally unsatisfactory'[15] the case for episcopacy ('as it developed historically in the early church') as the uniquely appropriate form of ministry. Even to speak of the episcopate, in a Cyprianic rather than Augustinian sense, as the *esse* of the universal

Church, raises fears (as in the Anglican–Methodist conversations) of the repudiation of other, even biblical, forms of ministry.

As I read the book again, I also wondered about some of the biblical exegesis. Was Ramsey in his argument making a theological virtue out of the necessary fact of division? Is it saying that disunity is not really the fault of man, but ultimately God's purpose? Is not this the kind of argument that Paul repudiates in Romans 6:1? And, in a politically sensitive area of Jewish–Christian conversations, is Ramsey maintaining that Israel's failure and supercession is a necessary premise of Christianity? The issue here is the problem of generalizing, of establishing absolutes and eliminating the inconsistencies between biblical texts.

Ramsey's next book, written during the war years, while he was Van Mildert Professor at Durham University, was *The Resurrection of Christ: An Essay in Biblical Theology*, published in 1945. The fundamental influence of Edwyn Hoskyns is formally recorded in the opening paragraph of the book:

> The writer of this book remembers receiving something of a shock when it was first his privilege to attend the lectures of the late Sir Edwyn Hoskyns. The lecturer began with the declaration that as our subject was the Theology and Ethics of the New Testament we must begin with the passages about the Resurrection. It seemed to contradict all the obvious preconceptions. Was it not right to trace first the beginnings of the ministry of Jesus, the events of His life and the words of His teaching? Here, surely, the essence of the Gospel might be found, and as a finale the Resurrection comes so as to seal and confirm the message. No. The Resurrection is a true starting-place for the study of the making and the meaning of the New Testament.[16]

The declared purpose of this book, as first published, was to investigate the place of the resurrection of Christ in apostolic preaching and theology, and 'to discuss the historical character of the event'.

The Resurrection of Christ is the point where the paths of History and Theology meet in a way that is crucial for the understanding of both. . . . I shall not be surprised if I am told that my treatment of the history is vitiated by presuppositions or that my exposition of the doctrine is cramped by the use of historical criticism. . . . In this book I have striven to combine the use of critical methods with but one modest presupposition, namely that the historical event was such as to account for the Theology of Resurrection which runs through the New Testament.[17]

Ramsey maintained a keen sense of the need for this balancing act between history and theology. He quotes extensively from Barth's commentary on Romans about the revelatory theology of resurrection; but he begins to dissent from the Barthians, and hark back to B. F. Westcott, if anyone should suggest that the examination of historical evidence plays no part in the resurrection faith.[18] Critics disagreed as to how successful Ramsey was in keeping the balance. C. F. Evans, a pupil of Ramsey, much preferred the theological chapters.

The passage of time can be noted in the revised edition of this book, published in 1961. It is not that Ramsey changes, so much as that the world has changed around him. There is a different subtitle: *A Study of the Event and its meaning for Christian Faith*. This failing of the biblical theology movement has caused Ramsey to distance his work from such a title, and also to substitute 'Biblical theologians' for 'Barthians' in Chapter 9. The revised preface concludes tellingly: 'The passage of time modifies the way in which the [historical and theological] questions need to be discussed. I hope that this book will help its readers to judge as to whether it alters the answers to be given.'[19]

Another book from the Durham days was *The Glory of God and the Transfiguration of Christ*, published in 1949. This was the book Ramsey said he was most glad to have written; certainly, it combines his theology and personal spirituality most closely. Again this work shows the Bible-centred nature of Ramsey's writing. The text is sprinkled with references to Old Testament key-words. The preface acknowledges a debt to J. M. Wilkie, a young and rising member of the Durham University department, for advice on the references. I am assured that Wilkie *did* spend a lot of time in correcting these references, but unfortunately the corrections were not actually incorporated by Ramsey – a fact which cannot have done Wilkie's career much good!

Between the preface and the contents, as one of three quotations, come these words from a Cambridge sermon by Sir Edwyn Hoskyns: 'Can we rescue a word, and discover a universe? Can we study a language and awake to the Truth? Can we bury ourselves in a lexicon, and arise in the presence of God?' The book itself shows the potential in the word 'glory' and, as Dr Kendall says, 'demonstrates Ramsey's power of biblical exegesis at its best'.[20] The first chapter concludes:

> Nowhere are the tensions of Biblical theology greater than in the doctrine of the glory. It speaks on the one hand of an invisible and omnipresent God and on the other of a meteorological phenomenon; on the one hand of Israel's transcendent king and judge and on the other of a presence tabernacling in Israel's midst. But in these tensions the validity of the theology of the Old Testament lies. 'Am I a God at hand, saith the Lord, and not a God afar off?' (Jer. xxiii, 23). Always in tension these contrasted aspects of the divine glory find their true unity when the Word by whom all things were made became flesh and dwelt among us, and the glory of Bethlehem and Calvary is the glory of the eternal God.[21]

The revised English edition of the 1967 contains a new preface about the dramatic change in the situation of biblical theology; it shows that Ramsey is still convinced of the importance of what he is doing, but sensitive to the new climate of scholarship.

> When this book was first written the linguistic study of Biblical words was very prominent in the work of theologians and

expositors. The linguistic method has been made familiar through the influence of the *Theologisches Wörterbuch* founded by Gerhard Kittel at Tübingen before the war. Linked with the method was the concern to expound the Bible 'from within', with a careful use of the Bible's own categories and an emphasis upon their uniqueness. The word 'glory' lent itself particularly to this method, for the many facets of its Biblical use have together a meaning foreign to its secular use both in the ancient and in the modern world. There was no exaggeration in the claim in the original preface of this book that 'the word expresses in a remarkable way the unity of the doctrines of Creation, the Incarnation, the Cross, the Spirit, the Church and the World-to-Come.'

Today the exposition of the Bible 'from within' is felt by many to be an unsatisfactory conception of the role of theology in face of the big gulf between Biblical and contemporary categories of thought and language. There is not only the challenge to expound the Biblical concepts in other categories, by paraphrase, parable and analogy. There is also the more radical challenge concerning the meaningfulness of the concepts themselves.[22]

It is important to include evidence from outside the scholarly writings as we trace the influence of biblical theology. A good and typical example from the preaching would be the *Sermon preached by the Bishop of Durham at his Enthronement on St Luke's Day, 1952*. This inaugural sermon is strongly marked by a sense of the continuity of Christian tradition, and especially the Durham 'vision'. Ramsey's first words as bishop were preached on the same text (2 Cor. 5:14) as Bishop B. F. Westcott's farewell charge to the diocese at the Miners' Gala sermon of 1901. It also includes two paragraphs which are typical of the inclusive statements of ultimate themes in the biblical theology movement:

'The love of Christ constraineth us, because we thus judge that one died for all . . . .' The love of Christ. It does not mean our love for Him, which is always a frail and feeble thing, but His love for us. *His* love: He is eternal God who came to our race in the great humility of the Incarnation, died for us on Calvary, rose from the tomb to conquer sin and death for us,

91

and now lives for ever, our Lord, unseen, present, contemporary. And now He is the head and we are the body, He is the vine and we are the branches: and as He gave Himself to us in the Incarnation so He gives Himself to us today: His flesh is meat indeed, His blood is drink indeed. . . .

The Kingdom of God does not advance in smooth and steady movement. If it did, we might be snared into thinking of it as a kind of worldly Utopia. There is no steady gradual advance of the good and retreat of the bad; wheat and tares grow together; the idea of 'progress' is not a Christian idea, and our Lord had no word for it. Rather does the Kingdom come in the ups and downs of love and judgment, of calamities and times of refreshing, of fresh disclosures of the power of evil and of the greater power of the Cross of Christ: yet come it does.[23]

To Owen Chadwick *Image Old and New* was 'the first considered reply to John Robinson's *Honest to God*'; to others it may have seemed a precipitate rush into print, and perhaps an over-reaction. But in these words radical denunciation meets pastoral sympathy:

This presentation of the deity of Jesus in relation to the Cross is novel in expression. But it seems to me to be in essence not far from the presentation in the Gospel of St John of the divine glory in the Cross. In the total self-giving of Christ in death there is shown forth the eternal unity and glory of God. While Dr Robinson sees the deity of Jesus in his deep-down relation to divine love, he suggests that the elements in the story which involve 'coming down from above', like the Christmas story, are myth. But he urges us not to tie up the deity of Jesus with the mythical elements, but to disengage it from them. Then the reality of the divine Jesus survives, even though the Atonement and the Resurrection are 'demythologized'. Much is left obscure in this treatment of the New Testament. Both the history which it contains, and the authority which it possesses, are left rather in the air. It is hard to see what firm ground is left. But, for our author, the deity of Jesus is made the more sure and intelligible by the line which he follows.[24]

Ultimately, the relationship between the archbishop and the Bishop of Woolwich was not severed, but grew into a learning process. Eric James, in his biography of John Robinson, writes:

> At the close of his thirteen years as Archbishop of Canterbury [he] wrote with great humility and candour in *Canterbury Pilgrim* that: 'I found myself a learner amidst the changing and unpredictable scenes of the 1960s.' He confessed his 'initial error in reaction . . . I was soon to grasp how many were the contemporary gropings and quests which lay behind *Honest to God*.'[25]

In *The Christian Concept of Sacrifice*[26] Ramsey provided a model of how he believed that traditional images should be handled. Historical reseach on the original meaning of the image is necessary, but not so that original meaning and Christian meaning should be simply equated. Nor should we jettison the imagery as antiquated and meaningless. Ramsey's prefered procedure is to ask: 'What . . . is new in the combinations made of these different imageries, and can we see in their new combinations and blendings the new creative Christian thing?'

An opening illustration recalls again the influence of Hoskyns, as does the recommendation to begin with the experience of the Apostolic Church rather than the gospel narrative:

> I remember one of my own great teachers, Edwyn Clement Hoskyns, many years ago saying that the concept of sacrifice has become spiritualized and etherialized: that we forgot what a horrible thing it really meant. He said that it would be a good thing if once a year a bull could be sacrificed in the college court, preferably on a hot summer's afternoon, just to bring home to all our senses what a horrible thing was this sacrifice that lies behind so much of the imagery of Christianity.[27]

The book *Jesus and the Living Past* had its origins in the Henson Lectures given at the University of Oxford in 1977 on 'History and Contemporary Christianity', which were then developed into Ramsey's second set of Hale

Memorial Lectures, delivered at Seabury-Western Seminary, Evanston, USA, in 1978. In contrast to the recognizable developments in thought between 1961 (*From Gore to Temple* – the first Hale Lectures in 1959) and *God, Christ and the World: A Study in Contemporary Theology* in 1969 – a book which shows the impact of some more radical theologians upon his thinking – these 1977–8 lectures are, in Chadwick's words,

> still the old biblical theologian of *The Gospel and the Catholic Church* or *The Transfiguration*; still with the conviction that to be a theologian it is indispensable to be a person of prayer, critical of theologians who said that you could not take a theology out of its cultural context, because great teaching has the power of reaching out across the frontiers of culture; and therefore radical changes in presentation or intepretation do not prevent an underlying identity in the faith that is believed and the gospel that is preached; and he did not think that the Incarnation could be for Christians a dispensable concept.[28]

The first Hale Lectures were a treatment of a theological era *From Gore to Temple* which ended at the Second World War; the second series is concerned with some of the theological questions that have dominated thirty or more post-war years. It is not in the same way an assessment of an era, partly because 'a fair appraisal ... must await a longer perspective of history'.[29] Yet the book's theme of Christian interaction with 'the living past' might suggest that the earliest Christians responded instantly and positively to their recent experience! 'There is a faith in the living past such as determines the hope for the future, and this faith is linked with the experience of a Christ who is believed to belong to past, present, and future alike.'[30]

Four questions about Christianity as a historical faith are selected for consideration: is the historical basis of the Christian story strong enough to take the weight of the Christian edifice? is the doctrine about Christ a proper inference from the Gospel? is a historical religion 'time-bound' by past revelation? and is the sense of the uniqueness of Christ compatible with worldwide perspectives including those of the other world religions?

Ramsey was experienced at responding to such questions clearly and helpfully, elucidating the question as well as possible answers and the reasons for his own convictions. Not all these questions were treated equally thoroughly or critically, however. Modern emphases were somewhat more obvious in the responses to the first and third questions, certainly in comparison with the second. Christian spirituality supplies an important element in the argument, on the grounds that it is 'a community of experience reaching across the generations' and it is not 'predominantly cerebral'.[31] But there is a missed opportunity here for a more stringent and modern critique of how closely this spiritual tradition can be linked to the historical events of the gospel.

At the end of this work (pp. 83–4), Ramsey quotes from his first book, written nearly forty-five years earlier. There are few writers, reflecting on a lifetime's experience and study, who could both affirm the truth of their 'youthful . . . audacity', and add, in a self-critical spirit, a whole new (eschatological) dimension to the argument.

Be Still and Know (1982) was Ramsey's last book. In its two sections it relates together the prayer of Jesus in the New Testament and prayers in the Christian life. Wakefield comments:

> Ramsey is ever the biblical theologian [as can be seen in] his exegesis of the verb which Hebrews uses in describing the prayer of the ascended Jesus, translated as 'intercede' but meaning 'to be with or to encounter, rather than to plead or speak or make petitions'.[32]

In conclusion, some attempt should be made to establish the strengths and weaknesses of biblical theology as practised by Michael Ramsey. There is no doubt that his writings have an inspirational quality and lasting appeal. His skill was to maintain a strict equilibrium between history and theology even at a time when the reliance upon history was being seriously questioned. He offered a mode of reconciliation between academic and spiritual concerns, because he had dedicated his life to both scholarship and the Church. The weight of responsibilities in Church leadership were no reason for him (any more than for his great hero Temple) to economize on his theological reading. And those hearers and readers who might have been uneasy with his tendencies to orthodox conservatism still found very compelling his sparks of theological insight and originality, his comprehensive and authoritative summing-up of issues and themes, and his powerful use of language and preaching rhetoric.

Michael Ramsey was committed to a programme of adult theological education. Evidence for this is everywhere in his writings, perhaps especially in the *Quarterly Review* he produced while Archbishop of York, and in his regular practice of recommending the latest scholarly books to the clergy and others. His own theology was essentially Bible-centred. For this reason it is scarcely surprising that he used the prevailing fashion of biblical theology, together with recent publications in the field, to promote study, discussion and debate.

A theology based on the Bible, essentially fashionable in the days of the biblical theology movement, provided a firm basis, a common ground to be worked over diligently, to benefit a wider scholarship and spirituality. But the 1960s brought questioning of biblical theology's presuppositions. It needed all Ramsey's wisdom and experience to steer the Church through an age of faltering confidence, competing claims and fashionable doubt. Essentially, he perservered in what he saw as his educational task, while listening to others and either moderating his own language in diplomacy or defending it in debate.

If one now attempts, at the end of the century, to place Michael Ramsey's writings in perspective, it is inevitable that the deficiencies of biblical theology are seen reflected in his work too. There is the tendency to isolate the Bible, as distinctively authoritative in its influence, at the same time as studying it within its historical context. Part of the problem is the limitation in knowledge about the biblical environment. We know substantially more now than was known in the 1950s about the cultural worlds of the ancient Near East and of the Roman Empire, but we pre-judge the influence of St Paul, for example, because we know more about him from the Bible than we know of other figures of his day.

Biblical theology exceeded available evidence by over-stressing the distinctiveness of biblical modes of thought. The pattern is reflected in the articles of theological dictionaries, where Hebrew or Greek influences contribute to the way our thinking is shaped, but the creative perspectives of Christianity, using other raw materials yet revealing striking new insights, provide the true climax. One danger at the end of this road is anti-Semitism.

The same model of theological dictionary betrays another tendency of this method: perhaps because the Bible is isolated and distinctive, it also seems to speak with a single voice of authority. The diversity of material in the Bible library has an unreal uniformity imposed upon it. There is a process of harmonization and theological synthesis, so that the differences between New Testament writers are softened. Perhaps all New Testament theology, including the Fourth Gospel, Hebrews and Revelation, appears with a Pauline cast of mind.

In itself, the historical critical process is laudable. Ramsey rightly stressed its essential value. Part of its ulti-mate deficiency must be the inadequacy of our knowledge, and the consequent dangers of selective presentation on the basis of what we think we know. But the other large problem with the historical method is what you do when you have 'established' the authentically original thought-world. Biblical theology, in the excitement of its explor-ation, often failed to recognize how alien the biblical world was from the modern one. Ramsey and others clearly recognized the need for an acclimatization process, if modern Christians are to appreciate the biblical world. But what if 'it is all so unimaginably different and all so long ago'? Might there not be some, or many, ideas that are quite incomprehensible in our contemporary philosophy?

Much of the time Ramsey was amazingly successful in his task of communicating such biblical ideas and attitudes. But the judgement of later generations on biblical theology must apply to him too. The imprecision of some of his working methods (however scholarly his aims) must cast some doubt on the validity of his conclusions.

Notes

1. For special assistance I record my gratitude to Richard Palmer, the Librarian of Lambeth Palace, with its Ramsey Archive, to Kingsley Barrett, and to Lorna Kendall and Robin Gill, the editors of this volume.
2. See Brevard S. Childs, *Biblical Theology of the Old and New Testaments: Theological Reflection on the Christian Bible* (London: SCM Press, 1992), and also the series *Overtures to Biblical Theology*, eds W. Brueggemann and J. R. Donahue (Fortress Press).
3. Robert Morgan, 'Biblical Theology' in R. J. Coggins and J. L. Houlden (eds), *A Dictionary of Biblical Interpretation* (London: SCM Press, 1990), p. 87.
4. Karl Barth, op. cit. Preface to the First Edition.
5. See Morgan, op. cit., p. 89.
6. Ibid., p. 88.
7. B. S. Childs, *Biblical Theology in Crisis* (Philadelphia: Fortress Press, 1970).
8. Owen Chadwick, *Michael Ramsey. A Life* (Oxford: Clarendon Press, 1990). p. 29. Ramsey's later reflection on Hoskyns is to be found in the Foreword to *Crucifixion–Resurrection: the Pattern of the Theology and Ethics of the New Testament* – the work of E. C. Hoskyns and F. N. Davey, edited by G. S. Wakefield (London: SPCK, 1981). p. xi.
9. Gordon S. Wakefield, 'Michael Ramsey: A Theological

Appraisal', *Theology*, XCI, no. 744, November 1988, pp. 457–9.

10. Ibid., pp. 459–61.

11. A. M. Ramsey, *The Gospel and the Catholic Church* (London: Longmans, 1936), p. v.

12. James E. Griffiss, 'A Classic Revisited: Michael Ramsey's *The Gospel and the Catholic Church* after Fifty Years', *Anglican Theological Review*, 69, 2, 1986, pp. 172, 174.

13. Ramsey, op. cit., p. 175.

14. James E. Griffiss, art. cit., p. 173.

15. Griffiss, art. cit., p. 175.

16. Ramsey, *The Resurrection of Christ: An Essay in Biblical Theology* (London: Bles, 1945), p. 7.

17. Ramsey, ibid., October 1944. Preface to first edition.

18. Ramsey, ibid., pp. 119–20.

19. Ramsey, op. cit., Michaelmas 1960. Preface to the 1961 Fontana edition.

20. E. L. Kendall, *The Mind in the Heart: Michael Ramsey, Theologian and Man of Prayer* (Oxford: SLG Press, 1991), p. 5.

21 A. M. Ramsey, *The Glory of God and the Transfiguration of Christ* (London: Longmans, 1949), pp. 21–2.

22. A. M. Ramsey, ibid., revised edition (London: Darton, Longman and Todd, 1967). Preface dated to the Feast of the Epiphany, 1967 (the earlier preface was dated Epiphany, 1948).

23. Text as printed in *The Bishoprick*, Diocese of Durham, December 1952, pp. 5–7.

24. A. M. Ramsey, *Image Old and New* (London: SPCK, 1963), pp. 9–10.

25. Eric James, *A Life of Bishop John A. T. Robinson* (London: SCM Press, 1987), p. 123, quoting from *Canterbury Pilgrim* (London: SPCK, 1974), pp. ix, 4.

26. Published as a pamphlet by the SLG Press, Fairacres, Oxford, in 1974 but given originally as a paper to the Anselm Society – a theological society he founded – in Canterbury.

27. A. M. Ramsey, *The Christian Concept of Sacrifice* (Oxford: SLG Press, 1974) p. 1. The lecture was adopted as Ch. 6 of *Jesus and the Living Past* (Oxford: Oxford University Press, 1980). See p. 64.

28. Owen Chadwick, *Michael Ramsey: A Life* (Oxford: Clarendon Press, 1998), pp. 410–1.

29. A. M. Ramsey, *Jesus and the Living Past* (Oxford: Oxford University Press, 1980), quoting from the Preface.
30. Ibid., p. 8.
31. Ibid., p. 19.
32. Gordon S. Wakefield, art. cit., p. 462, quoting from p. 73 of A. M. Ramsey, *Be Still and Know* (London: Faith Press, 1982).

6 Glory in Trouble: The Social Theology of Michael Ramsey

Kenneth Leech

There is no serious doubt that Michael Ramsey was a theologian of stature, and he has been called 'the one undoubted theologian to occupy the chair of St Augustine this century'.[1] But the view that Ramsey was a social theologian, that his theological thinking has consequences for social and political thought and action, would not be widely accepted. To many observers at the time, and to subsequent students, Ramsey was seen as a thinker whose attention was focused on the Church itself, on matters of ecclesiology, liturgy and apostolic order, or on the personal spiritual lives of Christians, and only slightly on the great issues of the world, issues of poverty, racism and human liberation. I want to argue that, while Ramsey was not a political activist, or indeed a political person at all, his theology is to be located within the tradition which goes back to F. D. Maurice and to the later Christian socialist thinkers; that his writings and his teaching were rooted in this social Catholicism; and that he helped to give theological underpinning, as well as spiritual and pastoral encouragement, to the work of more openly and more consciously political individuals and organizations.

The Gospel, the Catholic Church and the World

Ramsey wrote *The Gospel and the Catholic Church* as a response to the liberal theology typified by Charles Raven and H. D. A. Major, a movement of thought which was suspicious of creeds and sacraments and was inclined to separate the historical Jesus from the early Church and to make a sharp division between 'Christianity' and 'the Church'. Lay apologists such as G. K. Chesterton in *Orthodoxy* and Dorothy L. Sayers in *Creeds or Chaos?* were to attack the liberal movement at a more popular level. Ramsey's work was the first major attempt to show the inseparability of gospel, Church and sacraments. Within a short time it was receiving praise from reviewers. A. G. Hebert claimed that its great achievement was to have united the biblical and liturgical movements of renewal, while G. W. Addleshaw argued that it marked the end of an era of wandering in the desert of humanist theology.[2] John Robinson, writing nearly twenty years later, said that the book had 'confounded the liberals', while a Roman Catholic, preparing a doctoral thesis in the 1960s on Ramsey's theology, seriously wondered whether to devote the entire thesis to this one book.[3]

The Gospel and the Catholic Church was not only Ramsey's first book, but also (at 238 pages) his longest. In many respects it provided the basis and framework for his future writing and thinking. In it, he argued that the theological liberals were seeking to reduce and limit the Christian faith and to contain it within the confines of a specific cultural and intellectual period. In part, the book was an attack on such cultural captivity, and this opposition to 'cultural Christianity' was to remain throughout his life. He saw the gospel as challenging and confronting the current conformities of the secular mind. He claimed that

> the root error of the English 'Modern Churchman' is similar to that of the rigid Greek orthodox or the rigid Thomist. He is taking creed and dogma in a scholastic way instead of as a signpost to the Gospel before all scholasticisms, and he is isolating dogma from life and liturgy. But his real quarrel is not with 'ancient thought' but with the Gospel itself.[4]

Against this liberal reductionism, Ramsey asserted the foundations of both Church and creeds in the biblical revelation. His critique of theological liberalism is, in its essential features, applicable to the versions which are current today. Ramsey saw such liberalism and revisionism as both an unsure basis for life and faith and as leading in the direction of accommodation to the dominant values of the culture, including its political values.

The Gospel and the Catholic Church, while it does not address social and political questions directly, is an important text for understanding Ramsey's approach to these questions in at least four of its emphases. First, Ramsey claimed here that the Church was not an addition to the gospel but was itself rooted in the dying and rising of Christ. He rejected the liberal attempt to divide the historical Jesus from the Christian community, an approach which has helped to promote 'private' ideas of faith. Building on earlier writing (by Charles Gore and others) which had emphasized the Church as 'the extension of the Incarnation', Ramsey, in his opening chapter 'The Church and the Passion', spoke of the Church as the extension both of the Incarnation and the passion of Christ. Moreover, the Church, as a 'community of the resurrection', was itself an integral part of the evangel. 'The structure of Catholicism is an utterance of the Gospel.' Certainly there is no deification of the Church and no uncritical devotion to its magisterium. Indeed, he insisted that the Church stands always under the critique and authority of the Word of God. 'Catholicism always stands before the church door at Wittenberg to read the truth by which she is created and by which also she is judged.'[5] Yet, while the insistence on continual self-scrutiny and reformation is present, the doctrine of the Church is a 'high' doctrine: the gospel is social at its very heart.

This rediscovery of the doctrine of the Church is, according to Ramsey, a necessary element in the recovery of the wholeness of evangelical truth. He wrote:

the full recovery of the doctrine of the Church is bound up with the return of the Gospel of God. Catholicism, created by the Gospel, finds its power in terms of the Gospel alone. Neither the massive polity of the Church, nor its devotional life, nor its traditions in order and worship can in themselves ever serve to define Catholicism, for all these things have their meaning in the Gospel wherein the true definition of Catholicism is found. Its order has its deepest significance not in terms of legal validity but in terms of the Body and the Cross; its Eucharist proclaims God creator and redeemer; and its confessional is the place where man sees that in wounding Christ sin wounds his Body and where by learning of the Body they learn of Christ; its reverence for the saints is a part of its worship of the risen Lord. The claim of Catholicism is that it shows to men the whole meaning of the life and resurrection of Jesus.[6]

There is therefore in Ramsey's early thinking a stress on the gospel itself as social, as embodied in a visible and material social reality, and this stress was to remain with him throughout his life.

Secondly, Ramsey stressed the importance of the Eucharist, laying particular emphasis on its 'scandalous character' and its earthiness.

The flesh must be eaten . . . here in history, concrete, in fact, *Christos en sarki*. Yet history and fact have their significance in what lies beyond them. Like the Incarnation itself, the Eucharist is the breaking into history of something eternal, beyond history, inapprehensible in terms of history alone.[7]

This materialistic spirituality, this mingling of the concrete and the transcendent, was of central importance for Ramsey's spirituality. To what extent he was ever able to relate the theological vision to the concrete realities of human lives and political structures is open to dispute, but of his belief in the integration of liturgy and social life there is no doubt. It is interesting that, as early as 1936, he was praising the liturgical movement in the Roman communion and the growth of the Parish Mass among both Romans and Anglicans. Yet in neither communion did this become a mass movement until the 1960s. Here again Maurice and the later Christian socialists were of crucial importance, for, as Donald Gray has demonstrated, there was a deep gulf between those Anglicans whose Eucharistic theology was derived from the Maurician tradition, and those ritualists who followed the sacramental theology and practice of contemporary Rome.[8] Ramsey had no sympathy with the precious kind of sacramentalism which made a cleavage between the liturgy and the common life of society. He often quoted words from Arthur Vogel's book *Is The Last Supper Finished?*, words which summed up his own approach: 'Through the Eucharist we are extensions of Christ's vulnerability, sustained by the food of his victory; we are not guards placed at the door of his anteroom to protect him from profanation or contact with the world.'[9] Thus, in *The Gospel and the Catholic Church*, he rejoiced that 'the liturgy is being discovered, not as a mere exercise in piety, but as the basis of a Christian sociology'.[10]

Thirdly, the book had an ecumenical emphasis which was to help lay foundations for later developments. He drew on insights from Maurice and Barth, from Rome and Orthodoxy, and from Lutheran, evangelical and reformed traditions. In this, his work was one of the first English Anglican attempts to integrate ecumenical thinking into ecclesiology. E. L. Mascall, writing many years later, claimed that the approach to the role of the papacy in Hans Kung's *Infallible? An Enquiry* (1971) was virtually the same as that expressed by Ramsey in 1936.[11] It also indirectly helped to open up the possibilities for a new ecumenical theology, even though this did not occur for many years.

Fourthly, Ramsey stressed the Church as a new social organism, a transforming unit within society. This view was not developed in the book, though he did point out that the liturgy was being discovered 'as the basis of a Christian sociology', a term used by the Christendom Group for what we would now call Christian social criticism. It was his insistence on the social character of Christianity, expressed in the doctrine of the body of Christ, which led Ramsey to be so emphatic in his attack on individualism. 'Individualism', he claimed, 'has no place in Christianity, and Christianity verily means its extinction.'[12] It was his opposition to individualism, in spirituality as much as in socio-political life, which led him to be highly critical both of the spirituality of Thomas à Kempis's *Imitation of Christ* – 'individualistic through and through'[13] – and of the Counter-Reformation on the one hand, and, later, of the politics of Thatcherism on the other.

In considering the liturgical, ecumenical and social aspects of Ramsey's thought it is important to note the similiarity of his early work with that of a number of other studies produced in the same period. Two years before the publication of *The Gospel and the Catholic Church*, an Anglo-Orthodox symposium had appeared entitled *The Church of God* in which George Florovsky had stressed, in much the same way as Ramsey, the notion of Catholicity as integral wholeness, involving the transfiguration of personality, an idea which Ramsey was to develop in his study *The Glory of God and the Transfiguration of Christ* (1949). Again, it is difficult not to recognize the influence of A. G. Hebert's *Liturgy and Society* (1935), while Ramsey's own sympathy with the Christendom Group, founded a few years earlier, is evident in all his work.

Of equal importance was the way in which Ramsey anticipated much that was later to come to fruition in the Christian world. He saw the Second Vatican Council as a major vindication of the overall theological direction represented by his own thought. Much of his thinking about the social character of the gospel, the centrality of the *soma Christou* in New Testament thought, and of the Eucharist in the liturgical and social life of the Christian community is now accepted in most parts of the Church.

The Legacy of F. D. Maurice

While *The Gospel and the Catholic Church* was an attempt
to bring together biblical theology, ecclesiology and liturgical consciousness, the heart of Ramsey's theological position was the long tradition of thought and practice within
Catholic Anglicanism. This tradition had consistently connected gospel and Church, had seen the Church as a
constitutive element in the gospel, and had emphasized
the place of scripture within the Church. The attempt to
hold together a word-centred pattern of corporate worship
(morning and evening prayer) and an altar-centred one
(Holy Communion), with almost equal importance
attached to each, had created a liturgical consciousness
which was probably unique in the Christian world. Ramsey's early work certainly initiated a new phase of concern
for theological wholeness, but it was also a restatement of
the historic Anglican position. Again, in his integration
of scholarship and pastoral commitment, Ramsey was very
much within a long Anglican tradition which tried to unite
theology and pastoral ministry. In his teaching on the
doctrine of the Church as the Body of Christ, Ramsey
was very similar both to Lionel Thornton and to John
Robinson.

Yet within this Anglican framework, there was a specific
indebtedness to the social Catholicism of F. D. Maurice
and his successors. Maurice was probably not taken very
seriously as a theologian until Ramsey wrote *The Gospel
and the Catholic Church*. Among the theological influences on Ramsey, Maurice was particularly significant,
though there were crucial points where Ramsey's social
thought was in sharp conflict with that of Maurice. Maurice
was unsympathetic to the Oxford Movement, which he
saw as pietist and backward-looking, yet it was the fusion
of his theology with the Incarnational and sacramental
thought of the ritualists, seen most clearly in the work of
Stewart Headlam and Conrad Noel, which created a new
synthesis, Anglo-Catholic socialism.[14]

107

In his book *F. D. Maurice and the Conflicts of Modern Theology*, Ramsey saw Maurice as a healthy corrective to much Anglo-Catholic thought and also to the neglect of Creation and Incarnation which he saw in Karl Barth. The centrality of Incarnation in Ramsey's thinking is brought out in an article of 1945 in which he criticized 'the loosening of the Neo-Calvinists' hold upon the Incarnation as a central principle'.

> Partly this is seen in a failure to make that estimate of Man which the Incarnation demands. Partly this is seen in a readiness (observable in different degrees in some writers) to part with the idea of the Incarnation itself, since if all that is needed is 'an eruption into history for man's salvation', there is no special importance in the doctrine of God made man.[15]

Barth, however, had excited Ramsey, and he was probably the first non-English theologian to do so. Ramsey saw Barth as an important ally in combating liberal theology. It is probably true to say that there was no significant non-English influence on his thinking, other than the Orthodox and Barth, until the 1960s when what he described as 'the newer Ramsey' emerged.

There seem to have been two key moments which were turning-points in Ramsey's theological direction. One was 1940. His unease with biblical theology was related not only to its neglect of the Incarnation as a central principle but also to its lack of attention to the doctrine of creation. It was the stress on creation which came over very clearly in his University Sermon at Cambridge on 13 October 1940. A second turning-point seems to have been 1952, the year in which he began *The Bishoprick* in Durham. In his articles in this journal can be found a new emphasis on silence, retreat, and the need for a deep spirituality. Later one saw the fusing of the concern with the created order and with the spiritual life, not least in his book *Sacred and Secular* (1965).

It was Maurice, however, who, more than any other

single theologian, provided the framework for Ramsey's social thought. Ramsey saw Maurice as being particularly significant because of his rejection of the Fall as the basis of his theology, for his restatement of the classical view of the atonement, for his doctrine of the Church as a sign of a redeemed humanity, and for his view of the Trinity as the basis of a new social order and of what he termed socialism. For these and other reasons Ramsey believed that Maurice was a valuable guide for the Church in the twentieth century. In some ways, to understand the strengths and weaknesses of Maurice is to understand those of Ramsey. Both were Johannine thinkers, both had a strong belief in the glory of God and in the indestructible image of God in human persons. Maurice attacked those who made sin the ground of all theology and claimed that true theology was grounded in the social life of the Trinity. Both Maurice and Ramsey laid great stress on the glory of God, and both had a tendency to remain detached from, and give inadequate attention to, the minutiae of social and political life.

In a remarkable passage in his book on Maurice, Ramsey made a comment which holds some important clues to his own thinking. Noting that Maurice was seeking to resuce the idea of socialism for theology, Ramsey observed that there was only a small part of Maurice's theory which could be expressed politically. He went on to stress that

> Maurice was not concerned to sketch a vision of a Christian realm, or to place a Christian political programme: he is too apocalyptic in his thinking to paint pictures of a day when 'earth shall be fair and all her peoples one'. He sought rather to discover the Christian foundations of man's life in society; to say what this foundation is; and *to do certain things without delay* when his perception of the foundation demanded them. Do the will and learn more of the doctrine. . . . Such is 'Socialism'.[16]

This is, in fact, a fairly accurate account of Ramsey's own approach: he too was not concerned with political programmes, but deeply concerned with understanding the place of humanity in society, and, when he felt it was necessary, he undoubtedly did certain things without delay.

It was in the emergence of a radical social Incarnational and sacramental tradition that the legacy of Maurice was to make its greatest impact on Anglican thought. This tradition was to dominate Anglican theology from Westcott, through Gore, Scott Holland, Lionel Thornton and Frank Weston, to William Temple. It was this tradition which Ramsey described in his study *From Gore to Temple* (1960). In this book Ramsey saw Gore's *The Incarnation of the Son of God* (1891) as marking 'the opening up of a line of exposition of the Incarnation which was, in the main, to be followed in Anglican theology for many years to come'.[17] Anglican theology, he argued, owed much of its distinctive character to the central place of the Incarnation. A major part of this distinctive character was the tradition of social and political radicalism.

In relation to this tradition, it is perhaps fair to say that Ramsey was a critical supporter of its 'genteel' and reformist wing, and a warm admirer of its more radical and rebellious wing. He was probably never a member of the Christendom Group (when I discussed the matter with him he did not remember!) but he was certainly influenced by its thought, as he was by Conrad Noel and the Catholic Crusade.

'Christian Sociology' in Crisis

An important text for assessing Ramsey's understanding of Christian social thought is his paper *Faith and Society*, given at the Anglo-Catholic Summer School of Sociology in 1955. Here Ramsey noted the decline of 'Christian sociology': ' "Christian sociology" in this country is noticeably under the weather. The tradition of thought about the bearing of the Christian faith upon the problems of society has not in recent years been conspicuous within the Church of England.'

While the coming of the welfare state, itself a product in part of a whole generation of Christian thinkers, 'has appeared to cut the ground from beneath the feet of the Christain sociologist', Ramsey argued that a major factor in the decline of the Christian social movement lay in a theological decay, in the collapse of a theologically based social gospel, and he saw Billy Graham in particular as representing a new and dangerous individualism. He stood alone among the bishops in not only not welcoming Graham, but also attacking him for offering an individualized gospel which cut at the roots of Christian social action.

Warning that 'the preaching of the gospel has gone awry', as a result of appeals to 'less than the whole man', he cited Graham, the Inter-Varsity Fellowship and Moral Rearmament as examples of this distorted gospel. Nor was it adequate to welcome these appeals and then add to them a social dimension, for 'these forms of evangelism of themselves cut at the root of Christian sociology just as they cut at the roots of a rational faith'.

> The act of decision and conversion, instead of being related to man's place and duty in society, abstracts a man from his place in society; and society becomes the mere stage and scenery alongside which the moral decisions are made. The moral will is segregated from its context because the appeal is being made to less than the whole man as a reasoning being and a social being. So it is that fundamentalist evangelism helps to destroy the ground of a Christian sociology.

In this address Ramsey in fact claimed that Christian sociology was not simply 'under the weather' but actually dead: 'the aberrations in theology and in evangelism . . . together with the separation of theology from spirituality have been enough to kill Christian sociology'.[18]

It was the late 1950s and 1960s, his years at York and then at Canterbury, which saw Ramsey's entry into the

111

political arena. In a sense, it was an accidental overspill from his theology, for he was before all else a theologian and a pastor. As Archbishop of York, he preached at the Labour Party Conference in 1960. Stanley Evans, one of the best-known Anglican–Marxists, expressed his delight that this bishop, whom he had hitherto (wrongly) associated with the High Tory tradition, showed so much sympathy with the moral vision and aims of the Labour movement.[19] (In fact, this sympathy was evident in his sermons at Durham, including his sermon at the Durham Miners' Gala on the text 'Earth shall be fair and all her peoples one'.[20]) Ramsey's political role was mostly indirect. During his time as Archbishop of Canterbury he made few direct political interventions, but those he did make were effective and dramatic. Two examples were his statement, delivered to the British Council of Churches Assembly in Aberdeen, that the use of force to end the Smith regime in Rhodesia would not be contrary to Christian principles, and his strong attack on the racism of the Wilson government's Immigration Act of 1968.

There were three areas of political life in which Ramsey played a significant role, and they are worth examining briefly: his attitude to nuclear weapons and nuclear deterrence; his role in the campaign for homosexual law reform; and his involvement in race relations.

The Nuclear Issue

In the 1955 address on 'Faith and Society', Ramsey alluded to Churchill's understanding of nuclear deterrence as a 'redemption of horror by horror', commenting: 'I suspect that it has a theological basis, though I find it hard to formulate to myself what that theological basis is.'[21] He remained suspicious of nuclear theology. From his days at York, just after the early atomic tests, he was highly critical of those Christians, including at least two of his fellow bishops, who were preaching the 'better dead than red' thesis. He wrote in the *York Quarterly:* 'The thesis "better

dead than red" denies the power of Christians to endure
and to transform, and denies the power of a faithful
creator. It is appalling that such a thesis should have come
from any Christian lips.'[22]

During his years at York it is clear that he rejected
pacifism, though where he stood on the nuclear deterrent
was not so clear. He seemed, for example, to support the
British nuclear tests. Certainly, he was never a unilateralist, though he regarded deterrence as a dangerous basis
for policy, as he told the Canterbury Convocation on 19
May 1962. His position on nuclear weapons probably
helped to undermine some of the worst excesses of nuclear
theology among the bishops. His strong theology of
creation made acceptance of the policy of nuclear destruction unthinkable, and it is likely that, with the proliferation
of weapons and the increasing threat to the environment,
his thinking may well have moved more and more in a
unilateralist direction.

Homosexual Law Reform

In the obituary for Ramsey in the *New York Times* (25
April 1988) it was interesting to note that he was remem-
bered most of all for his support for homosexual law
reform. 'Support', however, is a weak word, for it was he
who led the campaign through the House of Lords, becoming extremely unpopular with some people in the process.
The Homosexual Law Reform Society, which eventually
became the Albany Trust, had been campaigning for some
years for reform of the law, and the Wolfenden proposals
brought the matter to a head. Antony Grey was secretary
of the Society and later of the Trust and saw Ramsey as a
strong ally and his speeches as 'a model of temperate
wisdom and charity'.[23] Ramsey did not approve of homosexuality, though he was deeply sensitive to the pastoral
needs of homosexual people, and it is said that at one
point five out of the seven members of his household
staff were homosexual.[24] It is possible that his strongly

expressed opposition to homosexual practice during the debates was a tactical way of winning his case rather than an accurate reflection of his own view. Nevertheless, for him the legal issue was not about the morality of homosexuality: it was about justice.

His support for this campaign led him into deep waters and made him unpopular with the Tory Right. To reread the debates in the House of Lords during 1965 and 1966 is a painful and depressing experience. Ramsey's first intervention was on 12 May 1965, when he announced his support for the Earl of Arran. While 'homosexual acts are always wrong', there were, he said, 'various degrees of culpability attached to them'. He was opposed to 'silly oversimplifications', and he supported the proposed changes in the law on the grounds of reason, justice and the good of the community.[25]

The following month he repeated his abhorrence of homosexual behaviour. It was 'abominable, utterly abominable', it had 'an unnaturalness about it which makes it vile'. Yet it was essential to consider the motives and the circumstances. Fornication could be just as abominable. He then raised a moral question which was to prove far more controversial than he perhaps anticipated. Referring to sodomy, he suggested that 'there are forms of homosexual intercourse every whit as disgusting as sodomy' but which were not subject to the same extreme legal penalties. Was there 'a big moral distinction', for example, between anal and oral sex? 'One hates to mention such things but by doing so one is perhaps able to clarify the issues.' He explained:

> I think the deep tradition of abomination of sodomy is utterly right, but I think the concentration on sodomy as the exclusively horrible sin may have been due in part to our very natural ignorance of the whole existing range of homosexual behaviour.

It was wrong he argued, for the criminal law to embody

a distinction which was neither moral nor rational. The disparity between types of offence was unjustified on moral and rational grounds.

Lord Arran was deeply impressed by Ramsey's courage and praised him. 'For the Archbishop of Canterbury to say in this House the things he has said is to me a very fine and a very brave thing.'[26] However, other noble lords were not so impressed. Lord Brocket, a peer of whom perhaps one would never otherwise have heard, attacked Ramsey for describing 'the various methods of doing this'. He went on:

I am told that Hansard of that day had an enormous sale. I believe it sold even better than the books on such subjects in the bookshops. I am sorry to say so but I very much resent that sort of thing happening as a result of our debates in your Lordships' House. I think it depreciates our position in the country.

Lord Brocket was particularly 'sorry that the things of this kind are brought up in this House by the leader of my church', and he later complained that all the bishops who came had voted in the same way.[27] But Ramsey was unrepentant. He had spoken frankly and plainly because prison sentences were at stake. He later pointed out that support for his case had been increased by 'a really lopsided presentation of morality' which had been given by opponents of the Bill.[28]

Race and Immigration Issues

As early as 1954, after the World Council of Churches had met at Evanston, Ramsey saw 'the primacy and poignancy of the question of race for the Christian conscience'.[29] However, few people at this time made connections with the growing problem of racial discrimination in Britain. After the Notting Hill disturbances of 1958, pressure for control of black immigration increased, and the Commonwealth Immigrants Bill was introduced in 1962. Ramsey's

intervention in the debate in the House of Lords led some
to ask whether he opposed the Bill or not. Lord Hailsham
said that he was not sure whether the archbishop was for
the Bill or against it.[30] It is therefore worth recalling what
he actually said in what was his first public intervention
on the subject of race and immigration.

The occasion was the second reading of the Bill on 12
March 1962. Ramsey conceded that the government did
not intend a colour bar (surely a serious error of judgement
in view of the evidence) but that it was concerned to avoid
'the growth of certain conditions in some towns'. It was the
'vicious circle created by prejudice in the housing market'
which had 'made a case for the introduction of the Bill'.
He then said:

> I do most earnestly hope that the restrictions imposed by this
> lamentable Bill, this Bill introduced with repugnance, this Bill
> which is indeed deplorable, will be short-lived, and that the
> episode will arouse in the conscience of our country a new
> determination to attack again the conditions which have led
> to the reversal of one of our country's great traditions.

Was Ramsey then saying that the Bill was necessary, and
that it was its necessity which was lamentable and deplorable, or that it was not necessary at all? When I inter-
viewed him shortly before his death, he expressed the view
that the Bill ought never to have been passed. Probably in
1962 he was somewhat innocent about the degree of
racism within government, and it was to be some years
before his awareness of the complexities of racial issues
grew as did his own involvement. Certainly, his expressed
hope that the 1962 controls would be 'short-lived' was a
vain one, for the 'temporary provisions' of the Bill have
been constantly renewed and strengthened, and have
formed the basis of control ever since.

On careful reading of the speech it is fairly clear that
he did not accept that the case for control was a strong
one. He spoke of the need to attack the conditions 'which

have created any case whatsoever for this proposal of restriction'. Yet there was no way in which housing inequalities and discrimination could be affected by immigration control. Ramsey said: 'I think it is the ambition of all of us that our country should be one where the restrictions imposed by this Bill could not be conceivably necessary.'[31]

In fact, the restrictive legislation of 1962 was strengthened by the government's White Paper of 1965 which has rightly been seen as 'the foundation document in the history of contemporary racism' in Britian.[32] However, the Wilson government which issued that White Paper was also preparing the first Race Relations Act, and one of the actions which went along with this was the setting up of the National Committee for Commonwealth Immigrants (NCCI). Ramsey was invited by Harold Wilson to be chairman of the NCCI and it became known as 'the Archbishop's Committee'.

The NCCI was created in an atmosphere of controversy and suspicion. Its information officer, Martin Ennals, claimed that by creating it the government had 'planted the seeds of destruction of its own discriminatory policy'.[33] In retrospect this is clearly a seriously exaggerated claim, as many pointed out at the time. Subsequent legislation has become more and more restrictive, and discrimination at the doors of Britain has continued to be seen as the way to reduce discrimination within Britain. Maurice Foley, the Minister with responsibility for immigration policy at the time, put the argument crudely and clearly: 'The situation was bound to worsen as the number of coloured people increased.'[34] Others pointed out that the White Paper itself would lead to a worsening situation. Ruth Glass, in a letter to *The Times*, claimed: 'It meets practically every one of the demands put forward by adamant restrictionists – from the Keep Britain White groups to immigrant control associations.' Warning that positive tendencies were now being reversed, she argued: 'It sets out a colour bar

117

adorned by some sanctimonious phrases about justice and common humanity.'[35]

Did Ramsey really not see that this was so? Was he naïve, or did his high view of human nature encourage him to believe that hearts and minds in government could still be changed, and that good could emerge from this? It is undoubtedly true that much of the resistance to government policy on race was anticipated by the work of the NCCI in those early years, and here Ramsey's role was a crucial one. Although – and he would probably have said because – he was chairman of the NCCI, Ramsey was deeply concerned at the effects on race relations of government policy on immigration. He was highly critical of the 1965 White Paper. It had, he felt, undermined the very work which the government had asked his committee to do. 'The work of integration is being hampered by bad feelings aroused by the latest White Paper,' he told the Lords in December 1965. There were 'ominous and unhealthy signs' in the country, not least of which was 'a recrudescence of white racialist organizations'.[36]

The secretary of the NCCI was Nadine Peppard. Ramsey always spoke of her with great affection, and it is clear that he relied considerably on her judgement, knowledge and advice. She has referred to the years before 1965 as 'the age of innocence' in race relations.[37] Perhaps Ramsey was an innocent, but Nadine Peppard believes that he was far from innocent as chairman of the NCCI and showed a remarkable and perceptive grasp of the issues. The role of the NCCI was 'to promote and co-ordinate on a national basis efforts directed towards the integration of Commonwealth immigrants into the community'.[38] In this it was the forerunner of the work now done by the Commission for Racial Equality, and it was ignored whenever it suited the government.

The weakness and ambivalence of the NCCI's position became clear in February 1968 when the Commonwealth Immigrants ('Kenyan Asians') Bill was rushed through Parliament in thirty-six hours. The NCCI was totally opposed to the Bill and came within inches of an *en bloc* resignation. The two Asian members did resign, as did two of the staff members. Eventually the Committee decided to continue, but relations with government had by now become very difficult, and an exchange of letters between Ramsey and the prime minister was printed in the NCCI Report for 1967. In fact, the NCCI was replaced by the Community Relations Commission under the new Race Relations Act, passed in October 1968. Ramsey was invited to be chairman but refused. His speech in the House of Lords on 29 February 1968 was one of his strongest attacks on government policy. The NCCI, he stressed, had not been consulted, and he thought this was 'very odd'. The government might actually have benefited from consulting the one body which they had set up to promote good race relations. The Bill had caused 'a good deal of dismay' and 'distrust' of Britain. Worse than that, it had created two levels of UK citizenship. Indeed, he claimed, it had made the whole idea of citizenship into 'a technicality devoid of living content'.[39] His words were prophetic, for it was this Act which paved the way for the disastrous British Nationality Act of 1981 with all the terrible consequences for citizenship which we have seen since then.

Ramsey as Social Theologian

How are we to assess Ramsey as a social theologian? He stood broadly within the 'Christendom tradition', bringing to it his own biblical radicalism, yet sharing its detachment from the realities of industrial life. He was sympathetic to Christian socialism yet critical of its tendency to equate the Kingdom of God with a new social order. On 29 June 1977, in a paper given to the Jubilee Group at St Matthew's Church, Bethnal Green, he indicated where he felt the future priorities for Catholic social thought lay. He spoke first about the Kingdom of God which he saw as the dominant theological idea for Christian social thought. Yet he saw some Kingdom theology as inadequate and misleading.

119

His understanding of the Kingdom of God was undoubtedly a social one, but he rejected certain ways of interpreting this social character. In 1936 he had been critical of Augustine's contribution to the view that Kingdom and Church were identical. 'The *De Civitate Dei* certainly gives the impression that the Kingdom of God is identical with the Church on earth.'[40] Ramsey's vision was one which embraced the whole of the created order. He was certainly deeply committed to 'secular' issues, and it is clear from his concern with such questions as the ownership of land, the future of states and other political units, and the changing attitudes to sexuality, that he was more open and adaptable in areas of social ethics than many bishops and Church leaders, though he remained very firm in his commitment to orthodox dogma.

Ramsey's social theology was Incarnational, sacramental and strong on glory. However, there are problems with such a theological perspective. In contrast to Gore and Temple, there was a stark contrast in Ramsey between the social theology which he espoused and the practical politics which might bring about the desired result. Unlike Temple, he was not connected, in any long-term way, with any 'movement'. His speeches to organizations were not calls to militant commitment and action but rather invitations to think things through. This seems to point to the conclusion that changing society was not his primary concern. Valerie Pitt has helpfully suggested that a central weakness in Ramsey's approach was that he failed to set Kingsley's *Cheap Clothes and Nasty* beside Maurice's *The Kingdom of Christ*.[41] So much of his contribution to social thought was marked by the very transcendental character which he had criticized in Barth. His stress on the glory often failed to connect in any concrete way with the troubles of the world, so glory itself got into trouble when abstracted from the mess and concreteness of life on earth.

A major part of the problem was the fact that Ramsey was a 'pure theologian', living in a self-sufficient world which was both intellectual and spiritual. From this world he was able from time to time to utter prophetic statements. His liberal background reinforced his moral indignation and anger against injustice – against black people, homosexuals and so on. But his moral indignation had no backup in social theory, no analysis of society, no understanding of working-class life. A crucial weakness lay in his liberal assumption that change could be achieved without significant conflict. His own cultural background and his theological commitment to glory helped to insulate him from concrete engagement and from the political nuts and bolts of real life.

Yet somewhere within Ramsey was a spirit of profound suspicion and questioning not only of the Church of England (towards which he had a somewhat whimsical attitude) but also of the whole structure of society. How committed was he to the establishment and to the kind of Constantinian view of Church–State relations which dominates mainstream Anglican thought and practice? By the 1980s Ramsey seemed to have become totally committed to disestablishment. The Tractarian emphasis on the spiritual autonomy of the Church had triumphed. The individualism and inhumanity of the Thatcher years made him very angry indeed. As bishop and archbishop, his approach to the political order was in many ways naïve and innocent, yet deeply prophetic. He simply did not understand how political structures worked, nor was he interested in them. Hence his utterances, powerful and effective as they were, had no context. His was a voice addressed to whoever would hear. That voice will continue to be heard.

Notes

1. Gordon Wakefield in *Theology* 91 (November 1988), p. 455. I do not regard Don Cupitt's claim that Ramsey was not a theologian at all, because theologians must be heretics, as worthy of serious attention. See Michael De-la-Noy, *Michael Ramsey: A Portrait* (HarperCollins, 1991), p. 99.

2. A. G. Hebert in *Theology* 32 (1936), pp. 308–9; G. W. Addle-shaw in *Church Quarterly Review* 122 (1936), p. 337.

3. J. A. T. Robinson in K. M. Carey (ed.), *The Historic Episcopate* (Dacre Press, 1954), p. 13; Donald McDonald, OFM, 'La pensée théologique d'A. M. Ramsey' (doctoral thesis, University of Strasbourg, 1968).

4. A. M. Ramsey, *The Gospel and the Catholic Church* (Longmans, 1956 edn), p. 133. Cited below as *GCC*.

5. *GCC*, pp. 54, 180.

6. *GCC*, pp. 179–80.

7. *GCC*, p. 107.

8. See Donald Gray, *Earth and Altar: the evolution of the parish communion in the Church of England to 1945* (Alcuin Club Collections 6, 1986).

9. Arthur Vogel, *Is The Last Supper Finished?* (New York, 1968), p. 64.

10. *GCC*, p. 177.

11. E. L. Mascall, *Theology and the Gospel of Christ* (SPCK, 1984), p. 26.

12. The term 'Christian sociology' seems first to have been used by A. J. Penty in 1923 and was later taken up by Demant, Reckitt and the leaders of the Christendom Group. However, according to John Atherton, the term was known to the Library of Congress as early as 1900. See John Atherton, 'The limits of the market' in Michael Alison and David L. Edwards (eds), *Christianity and Conservatism* (Hodder and Stoughton, 1990), pp. 263–84.

13. *GCC*, pp. 38, 168.

14. On Anglo-Catholic socialism, past and present, see the publications of the Jubilee Group, 48 Northampton Road, Croydon, CR0 7HT, UK.

15. A. M. Ramsey, 'What is Anglican theology?', *Theology* 48 (1945), pp. 2–6.

16. A. M. Ramsey, *F. D. Maurice and the Conflicts of Modern Theology* (Cambridge University Press, 1951), p. 47.

17. A. M. Ramsey, *From Gore to Temple: the development of Anglican theology between 'Lux Mundi' and the Second World War 1889–1939* (Longmans, 1960), p. 16.

18. A. M. Ramsey, 'Faith and Society', address to the Summer School of Sociology 1955. The paper appeared in *Church Quarterly Review* 1955, pp. 360–6, and in A. M. Ramsey, *Durham Essays and Addresses* (SPCK, 1957), pp. 41–8. Cited below as *DEA*.

19. Stanley Evans in *CSM News* 4 (Christian Socialist Movement, March 1961), p. 4.
20. *DEA*, p. 102.
21. *DEA*, pp. 41–2.
22. *York Quarterly*, December 1959.
23. Antony Grey, *Quest for Justice: towards homosexual emancipation* (Sinclair-Stevenson, 1992), p. 90.
24. Michael De-la-Noy, op. cit., p. 181.
25. House of Lords, 12 May 1965, cols 80–4.
26. Ibid., 21 June 1965, cols 301–3; 28 June 1965, col. 685.
27. Ibid., 16 July 1965, col. 411; 28 October 1965, col. 707.
28. Ibid., 28 October 1965, col. 716.
29. *DEA*, p. 83.
30. *Church of England Newspaper*, 16 March 1962.
31. House of Lords, 12 March 1962, cols 24–9. See *Church Times* and *Church of England Newspaper*, 16 March 1962.
32. Robert Moore, *Guardian*, 16 April 1988. See also Robert Moore, 'Labour and racism 1965–68', *Institute of Race Relations Newsletter*, October 1968, pp. 383–90.
33. Martin Ennals, *Tribune*, 18 February 1966.
34. Maurice Foley, *Guardian*, 9 October 1965.
35. Ruth Glass, *The Times*, 9 August 1965.
36. House of Lords, 6 December 1965; *Guardian*, 7 December 1965.
37. Nadine Peppard, 'The age of innocence: race relations before 1965', *New Community* 14 (Autumn 1987), pp. 45–55; Nadine Peppard, personal communication.
38. *Immigration from the Commonwealth* (Cmnd 2734, HMSO, August 1965).
39. House of Lords, 29 February 1968, cols 949–54.
40. *GCC*, p. 155.
41. Valerie Pitt, personal communication. I have drawn on Valerie Pitt's reflections in this and the following paragraph.

In preparing this essay I have been greatly helped by conversations and/or correspondence with Michael De-la-Noy, Paul Oestreicher, Nadine Peppard, and Valerie Pitt. Some of this material previously appeared in my pamphlet 'The Gospel, the Catholic Church and the World' (Jubilee Group, 1990).

7 Michael Ramsey and Pastoral Theology

Lorna Kendall

Michael Ramsey wrote his last letter as Archbishop of York in the York diocesan leaflet in June 1961. In the issue for the following month there appeared excerpts from a television interview that Michael Ramsey gave before he moved to Canterbury. His conversation with Kenneth Harris demonstrates concisely the connection he saw between pastoral care and theology:

Q: What might you be, above all?

A: I'm certainly a pastor, because I have an immense love and care for people. I'm also a theologian – that means a person who tries to study Christian truth very deeply, in order to try to bring it home to the people as simply and convincingly as possible . . .

Q: Many people wonder whether, in view of the fact that you are pre-eminently a theologian, you are a suitable person to be the hundredth Archbishop of Canterbury. What do you think?

A: A theologian: but I've always been doing pastoral work. I've worked in three parishes at different times, though not for a long time. In the ten years when I was a Canon of Durham Cathedral I was doing university work but I was also in touch with people of all sorts, trying to help them. I've never *not* been doing pastoral work for the last thirty years.

The integration of pastoral care and theological excellence in a life of consistent dedication and prayerfulness could be illustrated from his many books, from personal knowledge of his life and ministry, and from the books and articles that have been written about him since his death in 1988. These are the foundations of the judgements made in this contribution, but most of the citations will be made from less accessible material, namely the regular pastoral letters that he wrote as bishop to his three dioceses: Durham, November 1952–February 1956; York, March 1956–June 1961 and also the *York Quarterly* which he re-founded; and Canterbury, July 1961–November 1974.

As Bishop of Durham, Archbishop of York, and eventually Archbishop of Canterbury, Michael Ramsey had many and varied duties and responsibilities, but he saw himself primarily as pastor and theologian in the discharge of his episcopal functions. The fact that he saw no dichotomy between the role of pastor and theologian in the exercise of his episcopal office was rooted in, and emanated from, his understanding of the nature and office of priesthood within the Church. During the two decades of his ministry as a bishop he had witnessed the growth of secularism and scepticism. At the same time there had been within the Church much questioning, much searching for new kinds of ministry to supplement or replace the older patterns. In his letter to the Canterbury diocese in March 1971 he affirmed that this searching and questioning had been right but went on to say: 'But we need amidst it to recover and proclaim vigorously that the priesthood is a divine gift to the Church, bringing a divine authority for divine ends through Word and Sacrament. Let there be more teaching and preaching about the divine gift of ordained priesthood, and more prayer that love for Our Lord will bring to many the faith and humility to receive his gift and his call.'

Throughout his episcopate he gave much thought and care to fostering vocations to the ordained ministry and to

the substance of his ordination charges. To those considering ordination, to those being ordained, and to those whom
he called upon to renew their commitment, he emphasized
that ordination was a response to the call of Christ himself.
He often asked his hearers to ponder the significance of
the word 'call', in the questions addressed to each new
candidate during the Ordination Service in the Book of
Common Prayer, as to whether they think in their heart
that they be truly 'called, according to the will of our Lord
Jesus Christ to the order and Ministry of Priesthood'. When
a candidate knelt before him to receive the laying on of
hands he had done everything to ensure that it was the
conviction that Christ had called him that had led the ordi-
nand to be there. The response to Christ's call is made
with the heart, the conscience and the mind, and there is
much that can be done to help those whom God has called
to perceive it, especially by corporate and private prayer,
but the initiative is always with God. Hence Michael
Ramsey observed that it was unfortunate that all the efforts
within the Church to help men to perceive the call to the
ordained ministry 'have been given the misleading name
"recruiting"'.

Whenever Michael Ramsey wrote or spoke about the
nature of priesthood as essentially a divine call, it was not
difficult to detect that he was at the same time affirming
his own priesthood and continuously responding to his
own call, as when he wrote in *The Bishoprick* (the quarterly journal of the diocese of Durham) in May 1954:

> It is instructive to go back to Christ's own call of the first
> apostles and see there the divine method. He did not offer
> them a sort of preview of the work which they were to do; as
> if to say, 'here is a work worth doing with such and such
> conditions, and such and such results and usefulness; pray
> compare it with the usefulness of being a doctor or a lawyer'.
> It was essentially a call to *Him*, to be *with Him*, to share in
> His mission and ministry as He willed to share it with them.

The next few sentences are as relevant (if not more so) to

126

the state of the Church of England today as they were when he wrote them forty years ago. He continued:

> The Church today in its reaction against clericalism has come to emphasize that every Christian has a vocation, and that the ministry has no more a vocation than the Christian engine-driver or the Christian gardener; and there is a tendency to say in effect, 'all these are vocations, consider the ministry as an option among them'. This emphasis on lay vocation is utterly true and right. But it is wrong to let it obscure the fact that there is in the ordained ministry a distinctive relation to Christ. All vocations are from God; all alike involve a call to be Christ-like; all are equally sacred; but the minister of the word and sacrament shares in Christ's own ministry as apostle and shepherd. In the last resort the call is not to a profession but to *Him*; and men who are untouched by an ecclesiasticism which dwells upon 'the Church's need' are won by an evangelical realization of Christ summoning them to be with Him in His work as shepherd of souls.

As we approach the end of the twentieth century amid large-scale unemployment, technological superiority, consumerism, the separation of morality and religion, and the pluralism of an increasingly secular society, it becomes increasingly difficult to give a resonant connotation of meaning to the concept of *vocation*, even within the Church. This is especially challenging against a global backdrop brought into our living-rooms every day by our television screens where we are made aware of millions of people, who, by reason of war, famine or disease, of natural disasters or political oppression, have little or no chance to choose whether to live or die, let alone 'respond' to a 'vocation' or 'divine call'. In his books and other writings and in his spoken utterances, it was abundantly clear that Michael Ramsey was fully and constantly aware of the challenges to faith in much of contemporary society. His understanding of the relationship of the ordained ministry to the Church and the Church's gospel to the world and its problems was rooted in a deep Incarnational theology:

127

When God became incarnate as man his meaningfulness as
God came into its own. The self-giving, the becoming-man,
the suffering love were not additions to the divine experience
or mere incidents in the divine history. In becoming man,
God revealed the meaning of what it is to be God. . . . So, too,
in Jesus the human race finds its own true meaning.[1]

Hence it was that Michael Ramsey attributed so great a
theological significance to the transfiguration:

The transfiguration of Christ stands as a gateway to the saving
events of the Gospel, and is as a mirror in which the Christian
mystery is seen in its unity. . . . But the transfiguration meant
the taking of the whole conflict of the Lord's mission, just as
it was, into the glory which gave meaning to it all. . . . Confronted as he is with a universe more than ever terrible in
the blindness of its processes and the destructiveness of its
potentialities, mankind must be led to the Christian faith
not as a panacea of prayers nor as an other-worldly solution
unrelated to history but as a gospel of transfiguration.[2]

It is this gospel of transfiguration that the Church has
to reflect in its own life and communicate to the world.

A very large number of Michael Ramsey's regular letters
to his different dioceses were mainly concerned with the
pastoral direction and care of the parochial clergy, leading
and guiding them, exhorting and encouraging them. The
various aspects of his pastoral leadership exemplified his
belief, expressed in his inaugural address to the International Congress on Biblical Studies at Oxford in 1973,
that 'for the understanding of the gospel of Jesus Christ
and its presentation in any phase of history, the role of
the historian or theologian is never wholly separate from
the role of the pastor and the evangelist'.[3] In his enthronement sermon in Durham Cathedral on St Luke's Day 1952
he outlined what was, and what remained until his retirement as Archbishop of Canterbury in 1974, his understanding of the episcopal office, especially with relation to
the clergy:

128

Finding myself called to be your Bishop I want only so to rule, so to teach, so to minister the mysteries of grace, that the love of Christ may not be hindered but spread abroad. This day brings an awareness of the alarming difficulties before the Church of Christ: but it is not the moment to speak of these. We know them: we often speak of them. Rather is this the moment to *encourage*, for to those who will look at things in the constraint of the Cross of Christ and the Resurrection of Christ the ground of our confidence is sure as ever. Let me therefore charge you, it is my first counsel, to serve Christ in His Church above all else with *joyfulness*. Members of the Clergy, rejoice that you are privileged to teach His truth, to care for His people, to celebrate the mystery of His body and blood, and to know perhaps His patience and His suffering as you serve Him. Let the source and the spring of your joy come – not from your environment, not from the way things go – but from Him.

Study, the exercise of priesthood, prayer and pastoral care, were all essential and integral to the ministry of bishops and clergy alike in the care of souls which, as the order of service for the institution of a new incumbent puts it, 'is both thine and mine'. At Cambridge Michael Ramsey had been the student and admirer of Sir Edwyn Hoskyns, who, in one of his 'Cambridge Sermons', had asked the students: 'Can we rescue a word, and discover a universe? Can we study a language, and awake to the Truth? Can we bury ourselves in a lexicon, and arise in the presence of God?'[4] Whatever may have been the burden of diocesan administration and ecclesiastical politics, or the time taken by much travelling, or the duties and responsibilities of high office, Michael Ramsey managed to retain pastoral care and professional theology among his priorities and to see them as being interrelated. For example, in the first number of the *York Quarterly* which he re-founded in November 1956 he concluded a discussion of 'The Gospel of St John in recent study' with

a word about a problem which I have always found perplexing, having as I do an equal concern for the scientific work of the professional theologian and for the pastoral life of the Church.

The nightmare was the suggestion that the one Christ could not be the same as the other, that Christ as we had known Him was divided; and it is here that the recent studies have been more than reassuring. Critical science, after a century of ups and downs, is reaffirming very plainly what had been the intuition of the Christian Church ever since the Gospel of St John had been received into the Canon – that there is one Christ whom all the Gospels show to us.

The high regard which Michael Ramsey retained for academic theology until the end of his life can be glimpsed from the following amusing anecdote. Around the date of his eightieth birthday the present author asked him, if he could have back one of his 'top' jobs, would he choose to be the Regius Professor of Divinity at the University of Cambridge or the Archbishop of Canterbury. With characteristic raising of the famous eyebrows and explosive laugh he replied: 'I think I would have to be Archbishop of Canterbury; I don't think I'm quite up to the other one now!' Perhaps it was with a certain wistfulness that, some years earlier, he said jokingly at a gathering of academic theologians: 'I was a real turtle once.'

Michael Ramsey thought it to be of the highest importance that the clergy should read and pass on to their congregation the fruit of their study. To this end he recommended, reviewed and mentioned books to assist them in their own development and in their work in encouraging an informed and well-equipped laity. In the course of his years as a bishop, through the channels of his diocesan periodicals, he mentioned, recommended or reviewed some one hundred and fifty books, sometimes devoting a whole letter to this purpose. Space does not permit of further comment, but twenty years on it is fascinating to rediscover the books which he considered important between 1956 and 1974. The unbreakable link between pastoralia and theology is evidenced by Michael Ramsey's understanding of the bishop's twin role of shepherd and teacher. In his first letter to the diocese of Canterbury in July 1961 he wrote:

Besides being a Shepherd, the Bishop is a Teacher. His throne is not only the seat of a ruler: it is the chair of a teacher. It is for me, therefore, to share with the Clergy the task of teaching the Christian faith, and to serve them in the doing of it. To that end, I have in my Episcopate striven to keep time to address deaneries and clergy schools when asked, and from time to time take Quiet Days and Retreats. There are other things which I would try to delegate to others before these.

In the next paragraph of the same letter is to be found the very heart of Michael Ramsey's pastoral theology. He continued:

Shepherd and Teacher, the Bishop is also called to be Inter-cessor for his people. As Aaron entered the holy of holies, with the names of the tribes of Israel on his breastplate, so the Bishop is bidden to go apart with God, bearing his people upon his heart. We need as a Church to be deeply involved with the world around us, with a keen sensitivity to the conditions of our time. Yes: but we need also to be far more ready to go apart with God, waiting upon Him in quietness, and learning what is meant by the words of an ancient Christian writer: 'as the soul is in the body, so are the Christians in the world'.

Shepherd, Teacher, Intercessor: pray that I may serve you in these things in the name of Christ.

Just as there was for Michael Ramsey no dichotomy between theology and pastoral care, so there was no dichotomy either between theology and prayer. Called to leadership in a Church which traditionally lays great store by the lives and writings of the early Fathers it is pertinent to point out that he was, above all, a theologian in the ancient sense of the word, namely, 'one whose prayer is true'. When the Patriarch of All Russia paid a visit to Canterbury in November 1964 his prayer that the Arch-bishop of Canterbury 'might have many years to lead his flock to heaven' seemed to be particularly appropriate. As the role of shepherd and of teacher was one that the bishop shared with the clergy, so was the joy and privilege of leading their flock to heaven. It was Michael Ramsey's expectation that the clergy would be pre-eminently men of prayer and would lead their people in the life of prayer.

Very many of the archbishop's pastoral letters were directed towards the keeping of the Christian calendar according to the Book of Common Prayer. For him the seasonal commemorations were no memorials of past events but an ever-present experience of the greatest mysteries of the Christian faith. His diocesan letters gave him the opportunity to unfold with profound simplicity the theological, doctrinal, spiritual and pastoral significance of the great seasons of the Christian year, sometimes emphasizing one aspect, sometimes another. Over the span of his twenty-two years as a diocesan bishop he commented on the whole sequence of the Church's year. For him, liturgy came to life in observing the Church's seasons and the articles of the Creed became a living reality.

In December 1971, for example, he devoted his whole letter to a consideration of the meaning of Advent:

> Advent recalls us to the neglected truth that God is our judge. . . . The path of a nation's calamities is often a self-chosen path. The New Testament picks up this thought and deepens it: 'This is the judgement, that the light is come into the world, and men loved the darkness rather than the light for their deeds were evil.' The Church therefore must preach judgement.

He went on to show that preaching judgement does not mean scolding and condemning, but perceiving the balance between the mercy and judgement of God. Nevertheless, he insisted that 'only a Church which accepts the divine judgement upon itself can know God's mercy in its own renewal and revival for its work and mission'. With the acceptance of judgement there is hope, a theme which leads through the Collects for Advent on 'the road to a happy Christmas'. His Christmas prayer was that the divine humility would conquer the pride of man (December 1961).

There were several occasions when Michael Ramsey wrote at some length about the three stories connected with the Feast of the Epiphany, the wise men coming with their gifts, the Baptism of Our Lord in Jordan, the changing of the water into wine at Cana manifesting Christ as '(1) the hope of all nations, (2) the divine Son who fulfils all righteousness, and (3) the bringer of a new creation'. The next sentence captures the excitement and enthusiasm with which the archbishop observed the festivals: 'these are glorious doctrines in picture, evoking our worship and stirring our imagination'; but he goes on to say, 'they mean nothing except in terms of a practical expression in human lives' (January 1957).

Consistent with his doctrine of priesthood and the importance he attached to the ordained ministry, it is not surprising that the archbishop referred to the Ember days as 'Seasons of Opportunity' and asked that they would be used 'to call upon the people to pray and to lead the people in prayer for the clergy'. He asked that at these four seasons there would be 'intensive and careful prayer' for an increase in the number of candidates, for those in training for ordination, and for the clergy that they might 'by faithfulness and joy of their ministry bring home to others the meaning of the life of a priest as the joyful, sacrificial service of God and humanity' (February 1964).

In the television interview to which I referred at the beginning of this essay, in answer to a question as to how he felt about becoming the hundredth Archbishop of Canterbury, Michael Ramsey replied:

People ask, sometimes, am I in good heart about being Archbishop of Canterbury? My answer is, 'yes'. I'm going to it right gladly to carry out my duty. But the phrase 'in good heart' sometimes makes me pause because, after all, we are here as a Church to represent Christ crucified and the compassion of Christ crucified before the world. And because that is so it may be the will of God that our Church should have its heart broken, and perhaps the heart of the Archbishop broken with it, just because we are here to represent Christ and Christ's compassion. But if that were to happen it wouldn't mean that we were heading for the world's misery but quite likely pointing the way to the deepest joy.

It is not surprising, therefore, that we find many directions in his pastoral letters to the keeping of Lent, Passiontide, and Holy Week. The letter to the diocese of York in 1957 entitled 'The Goal of Lent' indicates and summarizes much of Michael Ramsey's theology and pastoral care, liturgical prayer and personal commitment in a remarkable unity and harmony. I quote the first part of it:

The appalling rush and busyness of our modern life makes it all the more necessary for us to make a careful approach to the *season* and the *story* of the Passion of our Lord.

When we try to go back in imagination across two thousand years of time to realize what happened on the hill of Calvary, we are baffled by the weakness of our imaginative effort. But we should start not by going back but by looking on. Jesus Christ is alive as our risen Lord. Start with the present fact of the risen Christ. In Him there is still the same heart of love which Calvary once disclosed, the same relation to sinners and to sufferers, and the same eternal spirit of self-offering. The wounds of Calvary still belong to the risen Lord. Look, therefore, not first back to Him across the centuries, but up to Him as He is. . . .

So throughout Lent we dwell upon the temptations of Jesus in the desert, the example of Jesus in his life, and the movement of that life towards Calvary – only and always in the light of His risen glory and presence now. Hence the Eucharist gives us the right perspective, for at that Eucharist we look back to the Last Supper and to Calvary while we look up, more immediately, to our great high priest in heaven, 'the lamb standing as it had been slain'. The Liturgy always brings us near to the Passion as we plead and intercede through Jesus Christ our living, present, priest and victim.

As in all his pastoral theology his considerations of Easter, Ascensiontide, Pentecost, Trinity and the Sunday Collects are all impregnated by his knowledge and study of the Bible. One Eastertide, for example, he wrote:

The God in whom Christians believe is in a special way the God of the Resurrection. In the first chapter of his first Epistle, Saint Peter, the first and most vivid of all teachers about the meaning of Easter (and no wonder!) says that God raised Jesus from the dead and gave him glory 'so that your hope and faith might be in God'. Easter showed Peter what sort of God his God was and is: the God who raises from death, the God who – when human possibilities are exhausted – acts beyond human asking. The women went to the tomb 'when it was still dark'. Our God is one whose light flashes upon the scene of man's darkness. I suggest then that the first chapter of Saint Peter's first Epistle might well be our guide in our thinking, our study, our prayers and (if we are priests or teachers) our teaching through the weeks of Eastertide. *(April 1970)*

The Epistle to the Hebrews presents Jesus as 'the High Priest of our confession' and spoke of him who by virtue of his priesthood 'ever liveth to make intercession for us'. It has been noted that Michael Ramsey saw the role of intercessor as one of the chief of his episcopal functions in the care of souls, one which he shared with the clergy and laity of the diocese. He often used his diocesan letters as a means of asking for intercessory prayers on behalf of particular persons, Churches, causes or needs. The range of his petitions included all the Churches and extended to the whole world. His requests for prayers included South Africa 'in the grievous state of things in that country'; the mentally ill; ordinands; religious communities; peace; ecumenical conferences which he had to attend; the Queen; teachers of religious education; the Vatican Council; local government; the Commonwealth; war in the Middle East and in Vietnam; and the Anglican–Methodist proposals; in the conviction that

no work of the Christians as the soul of the world is more important than their work of prayer: the bearing of the world's needs upon the heart in God's presence. It is thus that we bear in our hearts the people of Ireland . . . and the peoples of Pakistan and India in griefs and anxieties that really defy description. *(October 1971)*

135

In the cohesion of his life and work and in the resolution of the balance (if not the conflict) between the active and the contemplative, Michael Ramsey seemed to epitomize the counsel of one of the early monks in the Eastern tradition: 'Put thy mind into thy heart, and stand in the presence of God all day long.' This is only possible when there can be found a measure of external silence and internal stillness. So it was that he frequently counselled the clergy to make regular retreats as he did himself, and suggested that parishes should encourage their clergy to do this not as a luxury but of necessity:

> While the life of the Church expands with new and tremendous demands upon the energies of the clergy and laity, how will the spiritual strength come? It can only come from the deepening of the life with God. If we give our minds solely to thinking about the multiple problems which press upon us we can exhaust our spirits in the process. We are stronger to face the problems with freshness of heart if our souls are knowing the joy and serenity of a deeper communion with God. That is why the prayer of a priest is so supremely important, as the source of his ability to train the people in the way of prayer. *(November 1965)*

Michael Ramsey liked to use the story in St Luke's Gospel of the walk to Emmaus while Christ unfolded the scriptures concerning himself, ending with the making known of the Lord in the breaking of the bread, as 'showing the place of both Bible and Sacrament in Christ's dealing with us: "The two tables", in St Chrysostom's words, "from which Christ feeds His people" ' (April 1956). Much has been demonstrated already concerning the Bible and the sacraments as the paramount sources of the authority of his ministry. Two other aspects which are not unrelated must be mentioned. The mention of such matters as 'the awe and dread which ought always to have a place in our religion'; the keeping of Lent; atomic warfare; disparity in wealth between the nations; and many others led him frequently to ask, 'What says conscience?' The examination of conscience leads to the questions of guilt and sin.

One of the dominant keynotes in the fulfilment of his priestly office was to express the importance and need of self-examination, sorrow for sin, confession (especially sacramental confession), forgiveness and amendment of life. The archbishop made his own confession regularly and saw the ministry of absolution as one of the greatest of a parish priest's duties and privileges, and often made reference to it. He acknowledged what he considered to be the wisdom of the Church of England in giving people the freedom to choose either to confess their sins alone to God or to confess them in the presence of a priest, but of the latter he said:

> they do something which is thorough, costly, decisive: through the pain of the confession and the joy of the absolution given by the priest in God's name, they are brought near to Our Lord. Whichever way of confession we choose, we are *all* called to confess our sins to God with care and sincerity. *(March 1959)*

The following is characteristic of his understanding of the priest's part: 'As absolver the priest shares, on the one hand, in the broken heart of sin and penitence and, on the other hand, in the sorrow and joy of Christ who bears our sins and pardons them.'[5]

The frequent mention of matters relating to sin and forgiveness in his letters, sermons and addresses found succinct theological formulation, for example, in his book *God, Christ and the World*:

> If theology would avoid the dangers of a false secularization the sure safeguard is to keep at its heart the essential Christian attitudes of creature to Creator, of sinner to Saviour. It is when we have lost the attitude of the worshipper, of awe and reverence in the presence of the Other, and when we have ceased to ask forgiveness for our sins, that the line has been crossed. It is on this line that the crisis for secular Christianity is located.[6]

However much Michael Ramsey's pastoral care was

rooted in a deeply sacramental theology, he was deeply concerned that the Lectionary and the Psalms should have a full and proper place in the worship of parish churches, and laid it upon the clergy to see that it was so. Of the Lectionary he wrote:

> A Lectionary teaches us the obligation of the Church to Holy Scripture as a whole. We of the clergy are commissioned to use the Bible not in the spirit of an anthology from which each of us picks what he happens to like, but as a great and many-coloured pattern of divine revelation towards the whole of which we have a debt. *(November 1956)*

In a long letter concerning the use of the Psalter mainly for the guidance of incumbents in relation to alternative cycles in public worship, he included a passage of which today's Church would do well to be reminded:

> The chief need is for us all to have more thought and teaching about the Psalms and our use of them. Let the clergy teach the people about the Psalms, and let the people be eager to learn more about the Psalms which they use in Church. The Psalms are a spiritual gold-mine. Make some allowances for the limitations of the stage in history when the Psalms were written, it yet remains that the Psalms have a timelessness in their power to mirror the soul of man. *(December 1956)*

One of Michael Ramsey's much used quotations was from St John Chrysostom's homily on 1 Corinthians, where he avers that it is vain to come to the altar of the Eucharist unless one goes out to find the altar which is identical with the poor brother:

> The one altar is a stone by nature, but becometh holy since it receiveth Christ's body; but this other altar is holy because it is itself Christ's body. This altar thou mayest see everywhere lying in lanes and in market places, and thou mayest sacrifice upon it every hour. When thou seest a poor brother, reflect that thou beholdest an altar.[7]

It was axiomatic that Christians were called to serve one another in the fellowship of the Church and that the whole Church should fulfil its mission to the world in love and service. In the wake of the message of the 1968 Lambeth Conference underlining the role of the Church as the servant of God and mankind, the archbishop put it in a theological and pastoral context:

> The love for God whom we have not seen is tested in the love for those whom we have seen and no human need lies outside the range of urgent and imaginative Christian service. It is all too easy, however, for the idea of service to the world to become secularized, as if the Church existed to give the world what the world thinks it needs in the world's own way. So the service of the world must go with an emphasis upon the world's deepest, and often ignored, need – reconciliation with God himself and with the worship of God who is himself the God of human existence. . . . When, therefore, we try to make our own and pass on to others the message of the Church as Servant we must be sure what it means. It means that Christians are here to be like deacons serving every human need. They are also here to be people who know themselves to be owned by God, to have Him as their ceaseless priority and to know that there is a bondage of obedience where true freedom is found. *(November 1968)*

Michael Ramsey's whole pastoral theology was undergirded by a sense of the interchange between the earthly and the heavenly. Possessing the fellowship of the saints and angels,

> we *already* belong to the heavenly country. We are on its frontier whenever we lift our souls to God in prayer, whenever we feed upon Our Lord in Holy Communion, whenever we reflect His love in our actions. It is as those who belong already to the heavenly country that we are alert to our present duties, sensitive to the world's troubles yet serene in the way we meet them. (October 1961)

An appropriate note on which to end is his reminder to the students of Cambridge University that the goal of our

earthly pilgrimage is no less than the quest of heaven and
that the road to it is the road of selfless love:

> Do not be afraid of looking towards heaven, for heaven is the
> meaning of our existence as created in God's likeness for
> fellowship with Him. And the quest of heaven is very far from
> being a pious escapism, inasmuch as the essence of heaven
> is selfless love, the same love which drives you to go without
> your dinner to help a family which has no food at all.[8]

Notes

1. A. M. Ramsey, *God, Christ and the World* (London: SCM
   Press 1969) p. 100.
2. A. M. Ramsey, *The Glory of God and the Transfiguration
   of Christ* (London: Longmans, 1949), pp. 144, 146, 147.
3. A. M. Ramsey, *Canterbury Pilgrim* (London: SPCK, 1974),
   p. 15.
4. Edwyn C. Hoskyns, *Cambridge Sermons* (London: SPCK,
   1938), p. 70.
5. A. M. Ramsey and L-J Cardinal Suenens, *The Future of the
   Christian Church* (New York: Morehouse-Barlow, 1970),
   p. 59.
6. *God, Christ and the World*, pp. 106–7.
7. St John Chrysostom, Homily XX, 1 Cor. Migne. P. G. col.
   540, vol. 61.
8. A. M. Ramsey, *Freedom, Faith and the Future* (London:
   SPCK, 1970), p. 37.

8 The Place of the Liturgy in Michael Ramsey's Theology

Louis Weil

During the years immediately following his retirement from the See of Canterbury, Arthur Michael Ramsey, accompanied by his wife Joan, made six extended visits to Nashotah House, an Episcopal seminary in Wisconsin. Those visits, five for six weeks and one for three months, offered Ramsey the opportunity to return to his cherished early vocation as a professor of theology for candidates preparing for ordination. As Owen Chadwick comments on this period, 'Nashotah did for [Ramsey] what he had expected from Cuddesdon, and he gave to Nashotah House what he had hoped to be able to give Cuddesdon. . . . Ramsey always looked back on Nashotah House as a halcyon time and as the most important part of his retirement.'[1]

As Professor of Liturgics at Nashotah House during those years, it fell to me to consult with the bishop as to what specific role in the liturgical life of the seminary he wanted to take in addition to his daily attendance at the regular cycle of morning and evening prayer and the Eucharist. Ramsey indicated that he wanted to take his turn on the rota with the priests of the faculty and staff for presiding at the Eucharist, and it was decided that I would be assigned normally as the assisting priest on these occasions because of my awareness of Ramsey's needs and expectations. In this context I soon realized that, in spite of his identification with Catholic churchmanship, the bishop really had little concern about ritual matters with regard to the minutiae of liturgical details. During the Eucharistic prayer, Ramsey's manual acts were minimal and did not conform to any of the prescribed models of Anglo-Catholic practice, neither of the Anglican Missal nor of the Roman rite. These were not matters of concern to Ramsey; his engagement of the liturgical act was at a wholly different level, and I became aware through my close contact with him on these matters that Ramsey never fell into the trap of liturgical myopia, of being too concerned about the rite in itself, but rather with what the rite pointed to and sustained, the intimate unity between the community of faith and their God. In this regard, Ramsey's engagement of the liturgy was far more mystical than rubrical.

This perspective to Ramsey's liturgical temperament is helpful for setting the framework for his understanding of the place of the liturgy in the life of the Church. Ramsey's view of the liturgy is never narrowly clerical but rather broadly ecclesial in its foundations. The importance of the liturgy for Ramsey is always rooted in its power to manifest the nature of the Church as the people of God fulfil their vocation in the world. The goal of this essay is thus quite modest. In it we shall consider the aspects of the liturgical/ sacramental actions which emerge in Ramsey's thought with particular vigour. A separate and valuable project would involve the examination of the various official and pastoral documents issued by Ramsey concerning the liturgy to his clergy in Durham, York and Canterbury, especially with regard to preparation for and implementation of the Alternate Service Book of 1980, but our concern in this essay is Ramsey's ground-plan, the theological perspective which shaped his approach to particular liturgical questions.

The Church, then, is the starting-point, and for our purposes here it is Ramsey's first book, *The Gospel and the Catholic Church*, which will serve to indicate his foundational perspective. If it seems strange to draw upon a work from the beginning of Ramsey's career as a theologian, we may note that, in spite of its having been published almost sixty years ago, it is still regarded as an enduring contribution to theological literature and has been reissued twice since its original publication. Further, we should note that as a writer and lecturer, Ramsey was not primarily concerned with liturgical subjects. In *The Gospel and the Catholic Church*, Ramsey demonstrates an awareness of then current developments in the yet tentative liturgical movement, and indicates knowledge of debated issues in liturgical studies, but for these he clearly depends upon the work of other writers. Liturgy was not for Ramsey a field of personal investigation. Thus what is most important for us here is not to be concerned about Ramsey's comments on one or another debated issue, but rather to present his understanding of the nature of the Church as it relates to the primary aspects of its liturgical/ sacramental life. For that purpose, *The Gospel and the Catholic Church* yet offers an excellent source for Ramsey's thought since, as he describes the book, it is 'a study of the Church'.[2]

Before considering specific liturgical/sacramental issues as Ramsey views them in the Church's life, we may note that for Ramsey two matters regarding the Church are given particular emphasis: its relation to the gospel, and the importance of its unity (and hence the scandal of its divisions). The first is seen in an ironic passage in which Ramsey discusses what he calls 'two types of Christianity', the Catholic and the Evangelical, and laments their inability to understand each other and to recognize the complementarity of the values which each affirms. The Catholic tradition 'thinks of the Church as a divine institution, the gift of God to man, and which emphasizes outward order and continuity and the validity of its ministry and sacraments'. The Evangelical tradition, on the other hand, 'sees the divine gift not in the institution but in the Gospel of God, and which thinks less of Church order than of the Word of God and of justification by faith'.[3]

143

In the face of this conflict, Ramsey calls for a fresh approach in which he asks those who identify with the Catholic tradition, with whom he associates himself, to find a new language in speaking of the Church and its institutions, a language which does not depend upon legalistic and institutionalist images but rather one which sees the Church as the expression of the gospel of God. In this simple summons, Ramsey the Catholic churchman embraces the evangelical language of 'the opposing tradition'. If one is to claim the legitimacy of the historic institutions of the Church, Ramsey teaches, it must be on their relation to the gospel. 'What truth about the Gospel of God', Ramsey asks, 'does the Episcopate, by its place in the one Body, declare?'[4] This is a test which all the Church's institutions, including not only its ministry but also its creeds and liturgy, must be able to meet. In the end, every aspect of the Church's life must be accountable to the gospel and can have no authenticity apart from it.

In an appended note which Ramsey added to Chapter IV in the 1956 edition of *The Gospel and the Catholic Church*, he underscores this primary theme with New Testament evidence of the connection between the gospel and the life of the Church. There he states that it cannot be inferred from this evidence 'that preaching by word of mouth is the only way in which the Gospel is set forth, for many passages show that the whole life of the Church is to be a setting forth of the Gospel'.[5] Ramsey comments that the whole of the apostolic ministry, and not preaching only, is 'in the gospel', since the goal of that ministry is seen in its mission to all people to proclaim access to God in Christ, which, Ramsey concludes, is done through every function of the Church, 'and not least the Church's organic shape and structure'.

The second aspect of the Church's life upon which Ramsey places special emphasis is its unity. Ramsey's vision of the Church is ecumenical, the one Church in the whole world. The local community is not primary: 'the very word *ekklesía* forbids us to think of any merely local community'.[6] In this Ramsey identifies his view with the teaching of the Congregationalist theologian P. T. Forsyth (1848–1921), whom he quotes on this issue:

> The total Church was not made up by adding the local churches together, but the local church was a church through representing then and there the total Church. . . . It was one Church in many manifestations; it was not many churches in one convention. . . . The great Church is not the agglutination of local churches, but their prius; . . . the local church was not *a* church, but *the* Church . . . the totality of all Christians flowing to a certain spot, and emerging there.[7]

This identification with Forsyth is interesting because Ramsey, like Forsyth, had an ecumenical understanding of the Church which did not accord with narrow denominational identities nor even with party identities within a single tradition. Although, as we shall observe later in this essay, Ramsey does not develop his views on baptism with regard to the unity of Christians as fully as we find in more recent ecclesiological reflection, the implication is clear that the essential unity of the Church is formed through the one baptism and that divisions over questions about ordination, as important as they may be, should not be allowed to overwhelm the fundamental unity which all Christians share.

The reality with which Christians live, however, is a divided Church, and Ramsey sees the effect of those divisions upon every Christian body as a kind of 'incompleteness' which characterizes the life of each Christian tradition living in separation from others who profess the same faith. In a passage in which Ramsey takes a strong stand on the essential character of the episcopate in the universal Church, he raises an important cautionary perspective to those who would use the episcopate as a justification for the Church's division. Ramsey writes:

> All who are baptized into Christ are members of His Church, and Baptism is the first mark of churchmanship. Yet the

145

growth of all Christians into the measure of the stature of the fullness of Christ means their growth with all the saints in the unity of the one Body, and of this unity the Episcopate is the expression. It speaks of the incompleteness of every section of a divided Church, whether of those who possess the Episcopate or of those who do not. And those who possess it will tremble and never boast, for none can say that it is 'theirs'. It proclaims that there is one family of God before and behind them all, and that all die daily in the Body of Him who died and rose.[8]

Ramsey's profound commitment to the Church's essential unity thus enables him in a sense to relativize even an issue as significant for him as the historic episcopate: the unity of the Church which baptism creates is so fundamental to Christian identity that even those traditions in which the episcopate has been maintained are, as it were, wounded when that unity is broken. The purpose of the episcopate for Ramsey is as an organ of unity and continuity, not as a source of division. Later in *The Gospel and the Catholic Church*, Ramsey links this view to the celebration of the Eucharist:

The Eucharist celebrated in any place is the act of the one family as represented in that place; and the validity of the ministry and of the rite is bound up with its meaning as the act of the universal Church. Hence, when historic Christendom is divided, the meaning of its orders and of its Eucharist is maimed; no longer are they performed with the authority and the outward commission of the *whole* visible Church.[9]

When Ramsey writes that in a divided Church by that very fact the ordinations and celebrations of the Eucharist are 'maimed', he is affirming an ecumenical ecclesiology which imposes a judgement upon *all* Churches for their role in causing or perpetuating such divisions which are contradictory of the one Church's essential baptismal unity. No tradition is really let off the hook. No tradition can claim to be the one Church nor to excuse its divisive stance on the basis of having preserved some particular treasure of the Church's heritage. It is the universal Church which gives both meaning and validity to all sacramental acts, and our divisions impair those actions as expressive signs of the unity of faith which it is their purpose to signify.

Concerning Initiation, Eucharist and Ordination

Although Ramsey does not give enormous attention to the ecclesiological significance of Christian initiation, his comments on it always point to a strong sense of its importance. As noted earlier, Ramsey affirms that 'Baptism is the first mark of churchmanship.' For Ramsey, the underlying issue is the establishment of a relationship with God through Christ and the Spirit. But how, he asks, did this relationship of which the New Testament speaks come about, and how was it sustained? That relationship begins, Ramsey says, 'with the response of faith in Christ crucified, when the believer recognizes his impotence and failure and lays hold upon God's act of love for him in the death of Christ'.[10] This faith leads the convert to an identification with the death and resurrection of Jesus which is accomplished through baptism. Yet from the start, this is an ecclesial incorporation, not an individualistic religious experience. The life of the convert

> is brought into a new centre and a new environment, Christ and His Body. The response of faith has preceded the receiving of this divine action, the response of faith is continually needed in order to appropriate it; yet the Baptism is, like the Incarnation and the death of the Christ, a real action of God who recreates.[11]

In these words, Ramsey brings into focus his understanding of baptism as the sign both of God's action towards humankind and the role of personal faith as the necessary subjective response to God's action for us, and both these aspects brought together in the 'new environment' of the Church's life. As he writes, 'The fact of Christ

147

includes the fact of the Church. And this is not a novel speculation added to the original Gospel; it springs from that Gospel.'[12] Baptism is thus the sign not only of life in Christ, but life in the Church. The two are, for Ramsey, one reality, a life in response to the gospel: 'The life of a Christian is a continual response to the fact of his Baptism; he continually learns that he *has* died and risen with Christ, and that his life is a part of the life of the one family.'[13]

Our consideration of Ramsey's understanding of baptism would not be complete, however, without asking where confirmation fits into the initiatory framework for him. If we look to his writings, they offer little information on this subject. In *The Gospel and the Catholic Church*, in the context of a discussion of the New Testament material on baptism, Ramsey makes one brief reference to 'the laying-on-of-hands as its normal completion', without even using the familiar name of 'confirmation'. This reticence may reflect appropriate caution about a subject which is quite problematic as to its practice and meaning in the various Christian traditions, and even within Anglicanism itself.[14]

Yet in a personal experience with Ramsey on one of his later visits to Nashotah House, I had the opportunity to see what we might call his 'pastoral conservatism' on the subject of confirmation. In addition to the lectures which he gave to seminarians during the Nashotah visits, Ramsey was often asked to give addresses to other groups. On one occasion, at Nashotah, he gave a study day for clergy of the Milwaukee diocese. There was much turmoil at that time in the dioceses of the American mid-west over the recent approval at the General Convention of 1976, of the ordination of women to the episcopate and priesthood. The mid-western dioceses, often known as 'the biretta belt of the American Church', were an area of particular conflict over this decision. At one point in his presentation, Ramsey said that the American Church had made a significant change in Anglican practice which concerned him greatly. He paused, and then said, 'I suspect that some of

148

you may think I am referring to the ordination of women, but I am not. I am referring to your new rite of confirmation.' He then went on to say that the rite of the 1979 Book of Common Prayer had abandoned 'the traditional Anglican understanding of confirmation'.

I was stunned by this comment since I had served on the committee which had developed the new rite, and which we felt to be expressive of Archbishop Thomas Cranmer's theological intentions.[15] I decided not to respond to the bishop in public, but I asked to see him the next day and we discussed the problems concerning confirmation at length. I saw that his view was very much shaped by the British social and ecclesiastical context and that in the many years of his episcopal ministry he had found values in the customary practice which he feared would be lost, with nothing better to take their place.

For Michael Ramsey, the word 'liturgy' is pre-eminently a reference to the Eucharist. In *The Gospel and the Catholic Church*, the Eucharist receives significant attention, and as we have seen to be characteristic of his approach to sacraments in general, the meaning of the Eucharist is grounded in the paschal mystery of Christ's death and resurrection (and thus can be said to be the continuing expression of the baptismal identity). It is always an ecclesial act. He writes, 'the rite is a sharing in the life of Christ and therefore a sharing in the one Body which is His people. As in all Christian thinking about *tò sôma*, the Eucharist and the Church are inseparable.'[16] In his discussion, Ramsey refers to another Congregationalist theologian, H. T. Andrews, who in a chapter published in P. T. Forsyth's *Lectures* wrote concerning the place of the sacraments in the teaching of St Paul: 'To St Paul, therefore, the bread and the wine of the Eucharist are not merely emblems of the sacrifice that was once offered for the sins of the world; they are the vehicle by means of which the virtue of that sacrifice is appropriated by the participant.'[17] It is clear in Ramsey's discussion that the Eucharist is no mere commemoration of an event long past but is the instrumental means by which Christians participate in the abiding reality of Christ's paschal mystery.

That participation, as we noted above, is always within the ecclesial context. Ramsey affirms St Paul's teaching as it is 'driven home' in the words of St Augustine:

> If you wish to understand the Body of Christ, hear the apostle speaking to the faithful 'now ye are the Body and members of Christ'. If you then are the Body and members of Christ, the mystery of yourselves is laid upon the table of the Lord, the mystery of yourselves ye receive. To that which you are, answer 'Amen', and in answering you assent. Be a member of the Body of Christ, that the Amen may be true. [Augustine, *Sermons*, 272.]

Commenting on this passage, Ramsey says that 'the fellowship between Christians is not only a very close corollary of their acts of receiving the Lord's Body – it is included within every act of communion, for the eucharistic Body and the Body the Church are utterly one'.[18] This identification of the Eucharist with the Christian fellowship is not narrowly linked to local communities around the world. Ramsey writes, 'For the Eucharist is never merely the act of a local community, but always the act of the great Church, wherein the local community is merged.' It is in this context that Ramsey places the normative limitation of Eucharistic presiding to the bishops and presbyters whose role involves a representation along with the laity of 'the whole Church of God in history and in heaven'.[19]

In his discussion of the Eucharist, Ramsey gives a lengthy analysis of the use of the word 'sacrifice' as descriptive of the Eucharistic celebration.[20] The Christian use of the term starts from the sacrificial offering of Jesus Christ as based upon and yet transcending the ancient Jewish sacrifices as being the action of the Son of God, thus an eternal sacrifice, and yet 'uttered in time and history in the life and death of the Incarnate Son'. It is this action of Christ in human history, his whole offered life, which gives to Christians a means of approach and reconciliation with God. In the celebration of the Eucharist, Christians encounter that reality expressed in words and signs in which they may participate and renew in their lives. It is in this sense that the Eucharist is an act of sacrifice: it is the place in which the one sacrifice of Christ is encountered, not only through a mental act but in the utterly human experience of a shared meal, a sacred meal in which faith is both signified and nourished.[21] It is the action in which all Christians offer their lives in union with the one oblation of Christ. Again, Ramsey confirms his approach with the teaching of St Augustine:

> The whole redeemed city itself, that is the congregation and society of the saints, is offered as a universal sacrifice to God through the High Priest, who offered Himself in suffering for us in the form of a servant, that we might be the body of so great a Head. . . . This is the sacrifice of Christians, 'the many one body in Christ', which also the Church celebrates in the sacrament of the altar, familiar to the faithful, where it is shown to her that in this thing which she offers she herself is offered. [Augustine, *De Civitate Dei*, X, 6.]

This high regard for the place of the Eucharist in the life of the Church is accompanied, in Ramsey's theology, by a welcome flexibility with regard to matters of rite and ceremonial. There is not a hint in Ramsey of some preferred ideal rite for the Eucharist nor for the style in which it is celebrated. Quite to the contrary, he refuses to engage in liturgical hair-splitting. To a narrow attempt to identify the Eucharist with its origins in the Last Supper, he responds that the Eucharist must be interpreted by the whole vision of worship in the New Testament. In a similar vein, he says that problems concerning the context in which the Eucharist originated are less important than scholars make them out to be. The constant emphasis in Ramsey's discussion of the Eucharist is on the whole of Christ's work:

The meaning of Christ's actions is determined by the whole meaning of His life and work; and it is here that the *crucial* point with regard to the institution of the Eucharist lies. Its interpretation depends upon the whole interpretation of His ministry.[22]

And that interpretation continues to unfold in the Church as the Eucharist is celebrated with great diversity in the various traditions. Although there are common elements, there are great variations in the ways in which Christians keep the Lord's command to 'do this' – different rites, different emphases, different cultural expressions, different theories of its meaning, yet all sharing in the rich mosaic whose very complexity is a testimony to the power of the Eucharistic action to be the focus of the Church's life in every time and place.[23] The relation of the Eucharist to the gospel and to the whole of human experience is summed up by Ramsey in this moving passage:

For the fact behind and within the Eucharist is not the last supper alone, nor yet the last supper as interpreted by S. Paul and S. John, but the whole Gospel of the Name and the Glory of God in Christ. The rite has within itself something which disturbs and causes change. Perhaps one of the signs of this disturbance is the separation of the Eucharist from the 'agape' or 'love-feast' with which it was at first associated. Just as our Lord, in the awe and isolation of the Passion, was set apart from mankind so as to be the nearer to them by death, so also the Eucharist had to be set apart from common meals in an awe and mystery whereby its nearness to common life was to be realized more deeply. The Gospel which moulded the structure of the Church moulded also the form of the Church's worship. This worship was and is the Liturgy, the divine action whereby the people of God share in the self-oblation of the Christ.[24]

The various ecumenical dialogues that have taken place in recent decades have demonstrated a high level of accord among the various traditions in their respective theological understandings of both Christian initiation and the Eucharist. A major fruit of the ecumenical movement has been the growing awareness that even where differences in these two areas seemed irreconcilable, as in the case of infant versus believers' baptism, or with regard to the understanding of the Eucharist in terms of sacrifice, serious dialogue revealed that such differences could be understood within a larger theological framework as complementary rather than conflicting. But this high level of accord has not been found when the various dialogues have moved to the discussion of the ordained ministries and of ministerial authority in the Church. Here the issues are much more problematic because each tradition's understanding of ordination and of ministerial authority has been significantly shaped by its historical and cultural experience during the centuries since the major divisions within the Church (and here I am thinking particularly of the Church in the West) occurred.[25]

We have already observed, in our discussion of Ramsey's teaching on the Church, how he is led to move directly to the relation of the episcopate to the unity which baptism creates. For Ramsey, 'the Episcopate is the expression' of that 'unity of the one Body'. But his reference to the episcopate at this point leads immediately to the incompleteness of every section of a divided Church, whether of those who possess the episcopate or of those who do not.[26] We are thus faced with the anomaly that ordination, which is intended as a sign or expression of the Church's baptismal unity, is often, in the lived historical experience of the Church, a source of disunity and division. We also noted earlier, and it is related to our discussion here, that the Eucharist, too, is 'maimed' when it is not celebrated 'with the authority and the outward commission of the *whole* visible Church'.[27]

These perspectives offer us a useful frame of reference for a discussion of Ramsey's teaching on ordination. The context for Ramsey is always ecclesiological. All discussions of liturgy and sacraments are set within Ramsey's understanding of the nature of the Church. Ramsey points to the crucial impact of the teaching of St Augustine upon a shift from what we might call a baptismal to an ordination paradigm of the Church. Whereas St Cyprian had taught that baptism and orders are not valid outside the Church, Augustine abandoned this stance for the more lax view that both baptisms and ordinations are valid if performed according to the authorized forms, even if this is done within a schismatic body. Their full meaning could be realized only through restoration into the one Church, but they were valid, since God was their agent, and hence rebaptism and reordination were not to be required when such persons were reconciled to the Catholic Church. This more relaxed policy was Augustine's teaching, and it prevailed.

Ramsey is critical of this Augustinian approach, especially with regard to its impact upon the understanding of orders which has dominated in the Western Church. Whereas

> the Cyprianic view makes orders utterly dependent upon the Church and validity a part of the Church's single life in grace, the Augustinian view leaves room for thinking of orders as valid apart from the Church's corporate life and for the idea of succession by orders as a single and isolated channel of grace. . . . [Augustine's theory] severs the doctrine of orders from the doctrine of the Body of Christ.[28]

The most appropriate focus for us to use in considering Ramsey's teaching on orders, and more specifically his teachings on the episcopate, is the question of the nature and meaning of apostolic succession. It is, of course, a phrase with various and disputed meanings. For Ramsey, it is first of all the succession of bishop to bishop in the office of pastoral leadership which 'secured a continuity of Christian teaching and tradition in every See'.[29] Succession was thus a safeguard for the continuous teaching of the true gospel of Jesus Christ, as each bishop followed the teaching which he received from his predecessor. The episcopate is thus the organ for the continuity of apostolic teaching in the life of the Church.

154

The apostolic succession also involved a succession of function, 'of preaching and ruling and ordaining, which the Apostles had performed'. The bishops thus succeed the apostles in their relation to the gospel and to the Body, and this place is summed up in the bishop's role as presider at the Eucharist in the assembly of the faithful.[30]

The third aspect of apostolic succession which Ramsey notes is the most problematic: 'that grace is handed down from the Apostles through each generation of Bishops by the laying on of hands'.[31] Ramsey acknowledges that this meaning associated with apostolic succession has been the source of serious controversy among Anglicans. Much of the conflict over this understanding of apostolic succession in Anglicanism originated with some aspects of the teaching of the leaders of the Oxford Movement in the nineteenth century. In such writers as William Palmer (1803–85) of Worcester College, Oxford, we find a narrowing of the understanding of apostolic tradition from that reflected in the old High Church tradition set forth in the writings of such Anglican divines as Bishop William Beveridge (1637–1708), in whom we find no hint of a preoccupation with tactile succession. For Beveridge, the succession is a sign and instrument of the Church's continuity, wholly dependent upon the Spirit of God, rather than some kind of self-contained, automatic, or even mechanical instrument of continuity. For Palmer, on the other hand, the emphasis upon tactile succession and continuity achieved a narrowness of definition unparalleled in the Church's teaching on orders and, not surprisingly, led to the controversy to which Ramsey refers.[32]

Ramsey is more gentle toward the Tractarian teaching than I think is justified, writing that 'They were fighting for the recovery of a principle, and had sometimes to express the principle in a static and partisan way.'[33] Then, in a note referring to Yngve Brilioth's *The Anglican Revival*, in which the author criticizes the Tractarians' emphasis upon apostolic succession, Ramsey says that 'this emphasis (however narrowly it was first expressed) was the means whereby sacramentalism was taught as *historical*, and linked with the one historical redemption'.[34] So Ramsey's sense of identification with the Catholic movement in the Church of England allowed him to be sympathetic to a position which he did not himself espouse. For Ramsey himself, succession is always seen in its relation to the gospel and to the visible unity of the Church. He writes, 'the meaning of the Episcopate is seen, not in isolation, but in close connexion with the whole Body of Christ and its presbyteral and congregational elements. To sever this connection is to corrupt the meaning of Episcopacy.'[35]

It is with this understanding of episcopacy that Ramsey is able to conclude 'that the Episcopate is of the *esse* of the universal Church'.[36] But its essential role is obscured when it is considered in isolation from the total ecclesial reality, when it is corrupted into prelacy, and when it fails to proclaim that there is one family of God, a family created in each generation through baptism.

Ramsey's understanding of the liturgy and sacraments is thus a consistent expression of the fundamentally ecclesial nature of his theology: in the Church's sacramental rites, the Christian community engages and reclaims its faith in the Gospel of Christ, and renews its identity as his body. He writes:

> The Christian who seeks to remember the Gospel of God and to realize all that it implies finds in the Liturgy the reminder which he seeks . . . He will test the evangelical character of a rite not by its precise resemblance to the rites within the New Testament but by its setting-forth of the whole action of worship which is the New Testament itself, and the whole Gospel of creation and redemption. It is still the Messiah who gives thanks and breaks bread; and herein is still summed up the life of the Church, the Gospel of God, and the meaning of the whole life of man.[37]

Notes

1. Owen Chadwick, *Michael Ramsey: A Life* (Oxford: Clarendon Press, 1990), p. 387.
2. A. M. Ramsey, *The Gospel and the Catholic Church* (London: Longmans, 1956) (hereafter, *GCC*), p. 5.
3. *GCC* p. 7.
4. *GCC*, p. 8.
5. *GCC*, p. 54. See my discussion of the relation of the sacraments to the gospel in Anglicanism in S. Sykes and J. Booty (eds), *The Study of Anglicanism* (London: SPCK, 1988), pp. 51 ff., and especially pp. 71–3.
6. *GCC*, p. 47.
7. P. T. Forsyth, *Lectures on the Church and the Sacraments* (London: Longmans, 1917), pp. 60–4. (Our quotation is Ramsey's somewhat modified citation, in *GCC*, pp. 47–8.)
8. *GCC*, pp. 84–5.
9. *GCC*, p. 223.
10. *GCC*, p. 31.
11. *GCC*, p. 33.
12. *GCC*, p. 34.
13. *GCC*, p. 60.
14. A useful survey of these issues is found in papers presented at the Canterbury Congress of Societas Liturgica in 1977, published in *Studia Liturgica* 12 (1977), pp. 116–50; see also J. B. M. Frederick, 'The Initiation Crisis in the Church of England', in *Studia Liturgica* 9 (1973), pp. 137–57.
15. It is not appropriate here to elaborate on this issue, but the theological foundations for the current American rite of confirmation are presented in a document prepared under the authorization of the Standing Liturgical Commission, and written by a member of our committee, Professor Daniel Stevick, *Supplement to Prayer Book Studies 26* (New York: Church Hymnal Corporation, 1973.) The literature on the subject is extensive, and is most conveniently summarized in Daniel B. Stevick, *Baptismal Moments, Baptismal Meanings* (New York: Church Hymnal Corporation, 1987).
16. *GCC*, p. 105.
17. Published in Forsyth, *Lectures on the Church and the Sacraments*, p. 151.
18. *GCC*, pp. 112–13.
19. *GCC*, p. 113.
20. *GCC*, pp. 113–18.
21. The sacrificial nature of the Eucharist continues to be a

157

disputed question among Anglicans as well as in the larger ecumenical scene. Aspects of the debate are presented in Rowan Williams, *Eucharistic Sacrifice – the Roots of a Metaphor* (Bramcote: Grove Books, 1982) and Colin Buchanan (ed.), *Essays on Eucharistic Sacrifice in the Early Church* (Bramcote: Grove Books, 1984).

22. *GCC*, pp. 98–9.
23. *GCC*, pp. 110–12, *passim*.
24. *GCC*, p. 108.
25. It is interesting to note that in the convergence statement of the World Council of Churches, *Baptism, Eucharist and Ministry*, the third section on ministry is equal in length to the first two combined.
26. *GCC*, p. 85.
27. *GCC*, p. 223.
28. *GCC*, p. 154.
29. *GCC*, p. 81.
30. *GCC*, p. 82.
31. Ibid., loc. cit.
32. Ramsey is himself critical of Palmer, *GCC*, pp. 217–18. I explore the implications of the emphasis on tactile succession in regard to orders in Anglicanism in 'A Larger Vision of Apostolicity: The End of an Anglo-Catholic Illusion', in Gerard Austin (ed.), *Fountain of Life* (Washington, DC: Pastoral Press, 1991), pp. 183–97.
33. *GCC*, p. 215.
34. *GCC*, p. 216, n. 3.
35. *GCC*, p. 84.
36. Ibid. On this debate within Anglicanism, see K. M. Carey (ed.), *The Historic Episcopate* (London: Dacre Press, 1954).
37. *GCC*, p. 168.

9 Michael Ramsey's Response to *Honest to God*

George Carey

As a society we are not particularly good at handling controversy, and it must be admitted that the Church is little better. Contentious matters of faith are not always handled reflectively. The spirit of tolerance that allows others the right to maintain strongly held positions is sometimes replaced by the intolerance which leads to greater disunity. Are there then any lessons from the past that might help us to do our work better and perhaps suggest better models of tackling dissent in a creative way, remembering that debate is a mark of a living Church?

I propose that one episode from the life of Michael Ramsey offers us some rich insights in this field. Thirty years ago, a book was published which took many people by surprise, including Michael Ramsey, the then Archbishop of Canterbury. The publishers, SCM Press, had ordered a print run of only 6,000 copies of *Honest to God* but by the end of the day of publication the first edition was completely sold out. The front cover was a powerful photograph of the German sculptor Wilhelm Lehmbruck's *Seated Youth 1918*, which was reminiscent of Rodin's *Thinker*, and which evoked the image of a young person engaged in serious thought. The author, John Robinson, the young suffragan Bishop of Woolwich in the Diocese of Southwark, was a highly intelligent, scholarly man who specialized in New Testament studies. Those were times of heady change in the world and the Church. In 1962 the

© 1993 George Carey

159

Second Vatican Council had begun. The exploration of space was moving forward apace. On television, British society was amused, rocked and dazed by the irreverence of *That Was the Week That Was*, which made stars of David Frost and Millicent Martin and fools of the Establishment. *Honest to God* caught the prevailing mood; it raised important questions about the truth, place and relevance of religion in a secular society. It opened a debate.

Dr John Andrew, now Rector of St Thomas's Church, Fifth Avenue, was Archbishop Ramsey's chaplain at the time. I quote from a letter he wrote me recollecting the weekend when the archbishop received and read the book:

> His wife and I noted two things, both unusual in themselves; he didn't change as he normally did from his suit into his house cassock – he kept his suit on, saying nothing. We were witnesses of a profound theological tussle going on in his head. He was in the process of digesting Bishop John Robinson's theological preconceptions and weighing the book in the balances and discovering that it was wanting. I never saw him so profoundly upset in the ten years I served him as he was over that book. He would repent towards the end of his life for his severity towards it – having grasped more fully the truth lying behind Bishop John Robinson's surprising theological statements. . . . But I shall never forget that weekend of silence and charcoal grey.

Bishop Mervyn Stockwood, then Bishop of Southwark, also wrote in a recent letter to me that, in his retirement, Michael Ramsey said: 'I made two great mistakes in my ministry – the first was over Robinson.' Mervyn added: 'He never did say what the other one was!'

What then was the nature of this mistake? It was, I believe, primarily to fail to take account of the signs of the times; and to see that Robinson had struck a nerve.

Many will acknowledge today that *Honest to God* was not John Robinson's most profound book. It was written hastily by a man seeking to summarize and popularize some very sophisticated theology. Despite the fact that his primary field of theological study was not doctrine but the New Testament, he opened up for many the existentialist world of Tillich, Bonhoeffer and Bultmann. Its obvious virtue was that it was written with a passion for God; it was designed to help people make connections with the world around them. Robinson intended it to be a missionary book. The week before, *The Observer* trailed the book with the headline: *Our Image of God Must Go*. While Robinson was not responsible for the headline, it has to be said that the article following mirrored the contents. It was meant to disturb and shake. It did. The popular press inevitably made the most of it.

At this point, we should remember two things. Robinson was already well known. The Lady Chatterley trial had been enlivened by having a bishop publicly defending the literary merits of the descriptions of sexual intimacy. Thirty years ago the news media found the mixture of sex and religion as potent a combination as they do now.

Secondly, much of the controversy centred on *The Observer* article, rather than on the book itself. Many of those with the firmest and most definite opinions never read the book at all. Instead, *The Observer* headline alone caused them to believe that the Church of England had an atheist bishop. After his performance at the Lady Chatterley trial many were willing to believe anything of Robinson.

Hero or villain? The battle lines were confused. For the Free Churchman, Erik Routley, the book 'gave me more comfort, more encouragement and more sense that life is worth living . . . than any book I have read for years and years'. For others it was a dangerous, unsettling book. One writer put it in these terms: 'What the rank and file church folk are concerned about is not the Bishop of Woolwich's ideas but the fact that it is possible for a bishop to deny the faith and yet remain a bishop, drawing his pay from the Church.' One rural dean wrote: 'I have read your book. There is only one course open to you, honest to God, and that is to resign your bishopric and get out of the Church of England. So long as you remain, you are a stumbling block and an offence to all who have not your intellectual pride.'

But the bishop was not a stumbling block to all. A Canterbury woman wrote that for her the book had been liberating, giving her permission to think dangerous thoughts and still belong to the Church. 'It is just so marvellous to have all this coming from a bishop of the Church and having one's thoughts confirmed, not rejected, from inside the Church.'

The uproar was great. It was inevitable that the archbishop was going to be drawn into it. The private correspondence in the library at Lambeth Palace reveals his great desire to maintain the unity of the Church, to understand the bishop and to defend the faith. Let us look at the archbishop from inside his office and try to work out why he acted as he did in the weeks that followed.

We have already noted his turmoil. He was distressed and he was angry. Distressed to be landed with a problem which seemed to cut across all he was seeking to achieve and angry because of the heady emotions the bishop's book had elicited. He seized the opportunity to go on television on 1 April and there he repudiated John Robinson's central tenet about the way we think of God. 'The book', declared the archbishop, 'began with something very misleading. It really is a caricature of the ordinary Christian's view of God. When the ordinary Christian speaks of God as being "up there" or of God "being beyond" he does not literally mean that God is in a place beyond the bright blue sky. He's putting into poetic language, which is the only serviceable language we have, that God is supreme.' The archbishop continued:

I think he is right when he is trying to find out whether some new image of God may be going to help some of the people who are right outside Christianity and the Church. But it is utterly wrong and misleading to denounce the imagery of God held by Christian men, women and children, that they have got from Jesus himself, the image of God the father in Heaven, and to say that we can't have any new thought until it is all swept away.

John Robinson was hurt by his archbishop's attack. He wrote to Michael Ramsey on 2 April: 'I really am distressed that you should seriously suppose that I am unaware of the pastoral problem concerned. It is of course utterly untrue to say that I wish "to denounce the imagery of God held by Christian men, women and children".' He also denied that he attributed to ordinary Christians a 'literal' belief in a God 'up there' or 'out there', and cited the tremendous response to his book as evidence of the way the book had been used pastorally. He reminded his archbishop that he had offered to let him see the manuscript the previous summer but that the offer had been rejected. The letter ended significantly: 'I am grieved that fellowship between bishops should be reduced to exchanges on television and in the popular press. This', said the bishop, 'is another part of the pastoral situation that gives me concern.'

It is evident that the fault was not entirely on one side. But the pressure on the archbishop to be seen to be acting was clearly immense. He was worried by two concerns. First, that attempts would be made to declare the Bishop of Woolwich a heretic through the processes of Convocation. Secondly, that the bishop's views might be seen by those on the fringe of the Church to be the new orthodoxy. How he sought then to rebalance his initial reactions are an object lesson to us all. He had to act quickly. Within two weeks he had produced a splendid booklet, *Image Old and New*. Lambeth Palace Library has a simple message from Professor Eric Mascall, then a Professor of Theology at King's College, London, who applauded: 'It is the best thing that has come out of the See of Canterbury since *Cur Deus Homo*!' The Father Superior of Mirfield rose to similar heights of ecstasy: 'Apples of gold in baskets of silver!' he wrote of the booklet.

It was a typical piece of Ramsey theology – wise, astute

and inclusive. He sent it first to Owen Chadwick, asking for his comments. The archbishop's mood and approach can be gleaned from this unpublished letter of 5 April 1963:

> It is my present intention to have the enclosed tract published a few weeks hence, and while the questions it deals with are so big that one could properly spend months writing about them, there is a bit of urgency. A great turmoil is on in the Church with a lot of unwholesome witch-hunting and I am anxious to address something chiefly to the members of our own Church but also to anyone who will read it to deal with the problem in a way that is both theological and simple. I am particularly anxious that our Church should not be made to appear unwilling to face the questions at issue.

Owen Chadwick's reply was exemplary in suggesting how to deal with controversy. He wrote:

> I should myself have expected that the less said by you the better, since the more you notice JATR's book the more important it becomes! I nevertheless think with great diffidence that it would be better, so far as possible, to avoid any appearance of writing a counter pamphlet. You have sought to avoid this suggestion, treating JATR with fairness, moderation and sympathy. Yet I cannot help feeling that it would be still better to take out as many references as possible to *Honest to God* and simply give the Church your positive reflections upon 'God without Religion', the Incarnation and the Moral Law: especially our image of God.

The advice was sound and it was heeded. *Image Old and New* was a simple, scholarly and thoughtful booklet which outlined the Christian doctrine of God. It was an archbishop's statement intended to steady nerves and reassure people. But it was not an attempt to deny adventurous thought or bold and innovative ideas about God. In the final section Michael Ramsey gave permission to explore:

> As a Church we need to be grappling with the questions and trials of belief in the modern world. Since the War our Church

has been too inclined to be concerned with the organising of its own life, perhaps assuming too easily that the faith may be taken for granted and needs only to be stated and commended. But we state and commend the faith only insofar as we go out and put ourselves with loving sympathy inside the doubts of the doubting, the questions of the questioners and the loneliness of those who have lost their way.[1]

Image Old and New certainly did help the Church greatly when it was published, but there still remained the fear that a heresy trial would begin. Here our attention turns to the Diocese of Southwark and Ramsey's relationship with its bishop, Mervyn Stockwood. One journalist trying to describe the mood there at the time wrote:

London south of the Thames has become the Red Belt of the Church of England. Mervyn Stockwood, Bishop of Southwark, is mild enough himself but he enjoys the company of turbulent priests, and behind every other dog collar in the pulpits under his charge you will as like as not find a secet Aldermaston marcher, a furtive abortion-law reformer, or a militant campaigner for the Socialist Kingdom of God. That is the environment in which Dr John Robinson, suffragan Bishop of Woolwich (a division of Southwark) has written *Honest to God*.'

Mervyn Stockwood, as the diocesan bishop, was also caught up in the affair. He too launched into print and wrote an article for the *Evening Standard* in which he likened John Robinson's stand for truth to that of William Temple. The article angered the archbishop. He wrote to Mervyn: 'I do deeply regret that you should have gone on to what is sheer falsification of history in connection with Archbishop William Temple.' He then continued:

I am not sure that you realise how very great is the distress with which I have had to deal about this matter, distress caused less perhaps by the book than by the article in *The Observer* and the irresponsible manner of presenting the issues to the public. Not the least part of the distress has been the ecumenical region (both Roman Catholic and Methodists) where I have found the matter almost heartbreaking. However, whether you and I agree about that, and possibly we do not, there is now the issue of orthodoxy pending. I have been trying to my utmost to avert the discussion of the matter on 'orthodoxy' v. 'heresy' lines. That is one of the reasons I have written a pamphlet to be published next week, in which I try to help bewildered people to understand some of the questions and to avoid heresy hunts, whilst exposing things which I believe to be misleading.

The archbishop in this letter went on to state his position. He asked: 'What are my responsibilities and indeed yours in respect of this?' He mentioned three points.

First, that responsible leadership must maintain the central core of Christian belief. He rejected Stockwood's line: 'I find it impossible to take the line of your article which is to say in effect, "this book may be heretical; but in the long run that won't matter. Several great men have been heretical before". To say that is to abdicate responsibility as a Church with a doctrinal position. I am sure that on reflection you will see that our consecration pledges make such a line impossible for you or for me.'

Secondly, that in his opinion the book was gravely at fault in its theology and his dilemma was how to avoid a heresy trial. Such pleas that the book had 'value' were not enough. If he were asked if *Honest to God* were contrary to scripture and the creed he would have to say, 'that is honestly my view of the matter'.

Thirdly, that he was determined to find the proper place for freedom of thought within a Church which took doctrine seriously. 'But', he added, 'it is impossible for the bishops of what claims to be part of the Holy Catholic Church just to run away from their pledges, or else we cease to be a teaching Church and just become a club for the discussion of religious opinions.' The archbishop's frustration becomes apparent in his final sentence to Mervyn Stockwood: 'Any solution, any action or inaction now, is going to be unhappy in one way or another, and this need not have been so if there had been at the outset a sense of responsibility about these matters, all of which could have been foreseen.'

Things were now coming to a head, and the archbishop's speech to the Canterbury Convocation became the focus of public attention. The archbishop, following his private correspondence with Robinson, was very willing to concede to his assurance that he had not abandoned Catholic doctrine. He declared in his Presidential address that, 'the Bishop assures us that he upholds the biblical and Catholic faith and that the book is tentative and exploratory'. Nevertheless, the archbishop reproached the bishop for the method chosen to present his views to the public, and argued that Robinson's doctrine of God fell short of orthodox faith. In particular Robinson seemed to be telling the public that 'the concept of a personal God is outmoded and that atheists and agnostics are right to reject it'. The archbishop went on to say, 'I doubt whether any argument could show that the doctrine which so far emerges is properly the doctrine of the Church.' The archbishop's tone was moderate and sympathetic yet firm and just. A letter from the Prolocutor of the Convocation of Canterbury soon afterwards indicates that the archbishop's firm Presidential Address, together with his pamphlet, had indeed steadied nerves; the danger of a heresy trial had passed.

John Robinson, however, was not happy. In his view the archbishop had not represented his position fairly and in a private letter a few days after the address, which later found its way into a Press statement, Robinson made two points. First, that the book only made sense as a missionary book. He did not reject the notion of a personal God but his aim was to question whether the doctrine of a personal God had to be expressed in categories and images which were unreal for modern people. Second, Robinson contended that his book was compatible with the creeds and formularies of the Church and argued that 'to explore new ways in which the truths for which Athanasius stood may be communicated is not to quarrel with the truths themselves'.

Before we look at the implications of this episode for our times, one curious postscript may be worth noting. We have already seen how deeply Michael Ramsey himself was hurt and perplexed. The furore within the Church had taken him by surprise. He was amazed and further distressed when just a few weeks later on, David Edwards, managing director and editor of SCM Press, calmly wrote to say that it was his intention to publish a sequel to *Honest to God* in the autumn. This would include a restatement of the Bishop of Woolwich's position, alongside responses from various people, including the archbishop. Edwards asked to meet the archbishop for half an hour to discuss this with him. The archbishop's response was to the point: 'I am very grieved that you have this intention. The questions involved are very big theological questions of great complexity. They call for long-term constructive work whether by the bishop or by someone else. . . . I am the more grieved that you intend to publish again the debates which have happened within the last two months for they have inevitably been immature and confused debates in which theological issues have been intermingled with other issues ecclesiastical and emotional.' The archbishop's view did not prevail. In the autumn *The Honest to God Debate* was published but without the archbishop's contribution. He had distanced himself from the debate. So passed into history the controversial beginnings of a small book which eventually sold well in excess of one million copies and was translated into seventeen languages. Interestingly, on 21 May 1963, both the archbishop and John Robinson were together at Mervyn Stockwood's fiftieth birthday. They were able to mend fences, if there were any to mend, with the process aided, no doubt, by Mervyn's excellent wines.

We have looked at the debates between Ramsey, Robinson and Stockwood. I turn now to Ramsey's self-confessed mistake in failing to recognise the spiritual quest of many people at that time, that is, in failing to read the signs of the times. He wrote later: 'I rather supposed that the need was to reaffirm the coherence of the faith on familiar lines, albeit with greater sensitivity and persuasion. If that was my initial mistake, I saw after a little further reflection that there was in the background a widespread crisis of faith which cried out for another kind of spirit in meeting it.'

It is easy to judge with hindsight, but Ramsey himself regretted to his last days the way he had handled the matter. He knew he had over-reacted, even though he never wavered in his strong belief that the episode was a very dangerous one for the Church. John Robinson, had, in a remarkable way, touched the nerve of the nation and got people speaking about God. It does appear from the literature available to us that initially the archbishop became too defensive in asserting traditional Christian teaching.

What was the nature of this reawakening provoked by *Honest to God*? Owen Chadwick in his splendid biography of Michael Ramsey states that 'it showed gropings, conscious and unconscious, among many people on the periphery of faith. It needed more understanding than contradiction. It was not just a press hoo-ha . . . a world of half-belief and half-doubt, of searchings and questioning, was dug up by *Honest to God*.' What Ramsey was later to realise was that while the bishop's book did greatly upset some Christian people, for others the book was a sign that courageous thought, even dangerous thought, was possible within the established Church. Some of John Robinson's statements were extreme, but many of those who actually read the book were not unduly disturbed. I was a curate in Islington at the time and well recall reading the book and finding myself mystified by the reaction it was receiving in the popular press. For anyone who had read any theology many of its views seemed quite commonplace. I still recall the many opportunities to talk about God to ordinary Islingtonians afforded by the enormous publicity surrounding the book. Not once did I find that it encouraged scepticism or endangered belief.

In making this point, I am suggesting that Robinson was in fact more closely in touch with some of the needs of the time, despite Ramsey's real concern for the sensitivities of the faithful. Five years later the archbishop confessed that *Honest to God* had made a more significant impact on the nation than he had realized. He wrote:

Since the stirring of the theological waters some five years ago by Bishop John Robinson's *Honest to God*, theology in England has to a large extent lost what we can now see to have been a long-established insularity. It was perhaps that insularity which made some of us slow to grasp what was happening. It was not that some people called 'new theologians' were inventing theologies of compromise with the secular world; it was rather that they were trying to meet, often in clumsy and muddled ways, pressures and currents already moving powerfully in and beyond Christendom.[2]

We must now look at what lessons the remarkable encounter between two gifted men has for us. I offer four reflections.

The first is that the contributions of both Ramsey and Robinson to the faith of the Church were rich and profound although they approached their theology from different starting-points. Robinson began with the mind, with intellectual study and with questions. In listening to the signs of the time he ran the risk of being subsumed by the categories of secularism. Yet Robinson responded to the questions of the age in a way that few others had, and helped many in their faith. Ramsey, on the other hand, came to his theology through worship. The mood of *Image Old and New* is quite different to that of *Honest to God*. Here are not anxious voices from the world demanding that God should reveal himself but the calm, measured tones of traditional faith offering an interpretation of the Christian life soaked in spirituality. For Ramsey was never able to speak of God without speaking in the same breath of prayer; and he could never talk of God revealing himself without speaking of Christ; and he could never talk of

Christ without speaking of glory revealed in humility. Perhaps this was why Ramsey had such close links with the Orthodox – a spirituality with which Robinson never appeared to have sympathy. Historically Ramsey's was the more traditionally Anglican way, for our doctrine and our liturgy have always been closely intertwined, but he appreciated Robinson's approach as well. We learn from the example of these two great men to appreciate those who come to their theology down a different path from our own.

Secondly, this controversy raised the issue of how theological questions should be handled within the Church. The Anglican Church has always prided itself on being a tolerant Church, able to hold divergent views together by means of its comprehensiveness. Suddenly an issue erupted which threatened this comprehensiveness and which called into question the Church's theological integrity. It would now appear that both Ramsey and Robinson were seeking to 'guard the deposit of faith', but from different angles. The archbishop, as we have seen, feared that *Honest to God* had stepped beyond the acceptable limits of belief. Robinson was equally certain that this was not so. He believed that he still stood within the tradition of Athanasius even when he was questioning the received categories of Western Catholic thought.

The resolution of this conflict is an example of one contribution which Anglicanism is able to give to the wider Church, that is, the capacity to tolerate differences in understanding our common faith. This capacity has, I suggest, two theological foundations. One is the nature of doctrinal truth itself. A living faith can never simply be static. The faith 'once delivered to the saints' has to be appropriated and proclaimed afresh in each generation. Borrowing an image from the arts, a theologian can be likened to a performer of the classics. Maintaining the tension between the original text and the cultural setting of the production requires great sensitivity and insight. We

171

barely realize how we are innovating even when we are attempting to be traditional.

The other foundation relates to the place of dissent within the Church. We should not externalize dissent by precluding questioning. Dissent is essential to a healthy Church. This has been true since New Testament times. The faith acclaimed within the Nicene Creed is itself the product of controversy, and that same freedom to question is needed by each generation. Inevitably that exploration will at times touch on even the core of our faith. If this were not so, theology would hardly deserve to find a place within any university. Theologians, by creative thought and encounter on the frontiers of belief, run the risk of hurting the Church they represent, but we also stand to gain much from the treasures of thought they will bring home.

My third reflection concerns the role of bishops as teachers of the faith. Coming, as many of us do, from a background of academic theology we inevitably continue to question and explore, but our prime responsibility as bishops is to guard the faith and to teach it afresh to each generation. The Ramsey/Robinson episode suggests that there are times when the limits of orthodoxy become strangely blurred. John Robinson was passionately committed to the faith but just as passionately determined not to subscribe to interpretations which failed to portray the true mystery of faith. Yet in doing what he did he disturbed many.

For example, he thought that from within the security of a Trinitarian theology he could question the expression of belief. He believed that it was possible to hold to a Trinitarian faith without retaining its neo-classical form. Ramsey did not believe that was so. He questioned Robinson's thesis and believed it to be erroneous. He was not prepared finally to condemn it. In hesitating to do so he reflected a long-established tradition within Anglicanism. Charles Gore put it thus long ago: 'If the Church is wisely "liberal" it will draw lines as seldom as possible. But if it is at all true to its traditions and apostolic precedents, it must always appear as a body knowing it has an essential programme to preserve and therefore "drawing lines" where this treasure is in danger of being invaded.' The Church, Gore went on to admit, had often been too free in drawing lines, but was certainly mistaken if it drew none!

The need for the balance Gore was seeking is still with us. Seven years ago [1986] the House of Bishops published a statement entitled *The Nature of Christian Belief*. It reaffirmed their commitment to the core of that faith uniquely revealed in the holy Scriptures, and set forth in the Catholic Creeds to which the official formularies of the Church of England bear witness. It went on to say:

> We accept wholeheartedly our mutual responsibilities and accountability as bishops for guarding, expounding and teaching the faith to which God has led us to commit our lives, and for doing so in ways which will effectively 'proclaim it afresh in each generation', while at the same time distinguishing in our teaching the ideas of theological exploration from the beliefs which are the corporate teaching of the Church. There must always be a place in the life of the Church for both tradition and enquiry. The relation between them is not simple and never settled, and has always meant that there can be a proper diversity in the understanding and expression of the Christian faith.[3]

Although not a part of those discussions, I wholeheartedly agree with their conclusions. As a Church we should have the confidence in our faith and doctrine that allows open debate and that drives us back to fundamentals. We should have the kind of faith in God and his Church that listens to the wind of the Spirit as it moves in the modern world in which we live.

My final reflection concerns collegiality between bishops. John Robinson was surely disingenuous to protest that his intentions were merely missionary and that he was not denying any central tenet of the faith. The public who read either *The Observer* article or the book could be in no doubt that his intention was iconoclastic. After all, the Preface states: 'A much more radical recasting, I would judge, is demanded, in the process of which the most fundamental categories of our theology – of God, of the supernatural, and of religion itself – must go into the melting.' He must have foreseen that his 'recasting' raised issues that went far beyond the writing of another religious book. They involved his role as a bishop of a Church with a defined body of belief and his relationship with his archbishop. Although it is true that Ramsey had rejected an opportunity to read the text the summer before, it is sad that a book of such significance was published without a serious discussion of the issues before publication, and that both Robinson and Ramsey were taken by surprise when the storm broke.

The episode reveals the problems that can arise if bishops are not in the habit of anticipating contentious issues, of sharing their thoughts and then acting collegially by working through their differences together. In the *Manchester Accord*, published earlier this year [1993], we have seen what can be attained by bishops holding widely disparate views when they are prepared to listen, talk and pray together and also to work extremely hard to find a way through. This provides us, I believe, with an example of what can be achieved when bishops are determined to stay together even though serious issues may separate them. I long to see the Church as a whole reflecting this quality of unity.

Such collegiality then is in vivid contrast with the situation in 1963. John Robinson was a bishop with many remarkable talents. We are still in debt to him for his revolutionary thinking in New Testament studies, on the ministry of the laity, and the role of the Church in the modern world. He was never a radical in the sense of one who had cut himself off from the faith but he was a Christian radical who wanted to get to the roots of things. His impetuosity was forgivable; his enthusiasm was commendable; his individualism was regrettable. Equally, many of the problems encountered at the time could have been avoided if the bishops as a whole had shown a greater common commitment to collegiality.

In the final paragraph of *Image Old and New* Michael Ramsey writes so simply:

> It has been characteristic of our Anglican portion of the Holy Catholic Church to learn from episodes of human thought without becoming in bondage to them. . . . So today it is for us to be ready to find God not within the cosiness of our own piety but within the agony of the world and the meeting of person with person every day. But wherever we find him he is still the God who created us in his own image, and sent his Son to be our Saviour and to bring us to the vision of God in heaven.

There we have at once the profound thinking of a great Christian scholar, the authentic tradition of Anglicanism, and the unity of intellect, prayer, and witness which is theology at its best.

Note

1. A. M. Ramsey, *Image Old and New* (London: SPCK, 1963), p. 15.
2. A. M. Ramsey, *God, Christ and the World* (London: SCM Press, 1969), pp. 9–10.
3. *The Nature of Christian Belief* (London: Church House Publishing, 1986).

The Michael Ramsey Lecture 1993, Scarborough Lecture Theatre, University of Durham, Friday, 19 March, 1993.

10   Michael Ramsey – A Theological Speculation

Robin Gill

Archbishop George Carey's article in this collection looks at the *Honest to God* debate and the role of his famous predecessor within it. It allows us to read some of the private correspondence held at Lambeth and to appreciate afresh the deep theological and pastoral anxiety that the debate caused Archbishop Michael Ramsey. As a brother bishop he wished to take John Robinson's theological explorations seriously. That is clear. He wished to be sensitive to modern culture and society and remained troubled for the rest of his life that he might not have been in his debate with Robinson. But he also wished to 'guard the deposit of the faith' and feared that Robinson's was not the right path to do this. As George Carey shows, Ramsey and Robinson were indeed set on different paths, albeit trying to reach the same end – namely, that of commending the Christian faith to an increasingly sceptical age.

The questions raised remain with us today. Particularly crucial is this: In order to commend Christian faith today, is it necessary to prune it of those elements which seem incredible in the late twentieth century? Or is the proper way to live and work within the Christian faith in all its richness and peculiarities without ever pretending fully to comprehend it? If the first was Robinson's path, the second was Ramsey's. Of course, there is also a third path. This claims that the proper way to commend the Christian faith today is to present it as a set of clear propositions that challenges late twentieth-century scepticism. If culture today is increasingly sceptical about Christian claims, then that is too bad for culture, not for Christian faith. This more polemical approach was largely that of the other giant of the *Honest to God* debate, Professor Eric Mascall.

I have a special affection for all three theologians. As I mentioned in the introduction, it is a particular privilege to be the first holder of the Michael Ramsey Chair of Modern Theology. Eric Mascall was the kindly and diligent supervisor of my PhD in Christology. And three months after *Honest to God*[1] was published (and at the height of the controversy) John Robinson sent me a hand-written letter telling a nineteen-year-old that he had been accepted for ordination training. Each in his way acted as a theological mentor for me. As a theological student I was enormously excited by Robinson, before being schooled as a postgraduate more profoundly by Mascall. Yet slowly I have come to see Ramsey's path as the most appropriate way to do theology in a troubled age. In this essay I hope to show why.

To do this I propose to engage in a theological speculation. Perhaps somewhat unfairly, I shall treat Anthony Freeman's *God in Us*[2] as the modern-day *Honest to God*. Too much has now been said about the latter to add anything useful here. Instead, I shall speculate that Ramsey and Mascall are still with us as lucid nonagenarians. If they had lived beyond their eighties, how might they have responded to *God in Us*? At the end of this speculation I shall try to identify some of the key features that emerge from this imaginary debate.

There are a number of similarities between *Honest to God* and *God in Us*, as well as some obvious differences. Both books were published by SCM Press (albeit thirty years apart) with an expectation by the SCM directors that they might cause a stir. The fact that David Edwards, the SCM Press director in 1963, twice suggested (unsuccessfully) that Michael Ramsey might wish to read *Honest to God* before it was published shows that he was aware of its controversial nature. And the more radical John Bowden, the current director and long-time publisher of Don Cupitt, must have known that Anthony Freeman was an untenured priest serving in a traditionalist diocese. Although Cupitt has often been regarded as a litmus test of Anglican comprehensiveness, his high literary and philosophical terms, elliptical style and tenured university position have always secured his position from ecclesiastical sanctions. Anthony Freeman, in contrast, writes in frank and straightforward prose and had tenure neither in his diocesan post in continuing ministerial education nor in his parish.

For both Freeman and Robinson, albeit as priest-in-charge and bishop respectively, writing a controversial populist book effectively brought their Church careers to an end. Freeman immediately lost his diocesan advisory post and, a year later, his job as priest-in-charge. Robinson continued as Bishop of Woolwich for another six years, but at the end of it was strongly encouraged by Michael Ramsey and others to return to academic life.[3] The rest of his career was spent as Dean of Chapel at Trinity College, Cambridge, without any further promotion. Neither the professorship nor the diocesan bishopric that he had hoped for were offered to him.

Theologically, *God in Us* is probably closer to Paul van Buren's *The Secular Meaning of the Gospel* and to the work of Don Cupitt since 1980 than it is to *Honest to God*. But it does share with *Honest to God* a more populist approach than van Buren or Cupitt. And both *Honest to God* and *God in Us* locate God 'in us' or 'in our depth'. Where they differ – and this is crucial – is whether they presuppose that their immanent understandings of God exhaust all that we can say about God or not. For the moment at least, Freeman seems to believe that it does. He remains firmly committed to the Sea of Faith movement and apparently sees no room for transcendence in his Christian faith. Robinson soon wrote *Exploration into God*, in which he insisted that he did see a need for

178

transcendence. Like van Buren, but unlike Cupitt, once challenged by others Robinson denied that he had ever been 'trying to substitute immanence for transcendence, to replace the God "up there" or "out there" by one "in here" . . . for without transcendence God becomes indistinguishable from the world, and so superfluous'.[4] He died with enormous courage and dignity, and minutes before dying he recited his favourite Collect with Ruth, his wife:

> O God, the protector of all that trust in thee, without whom nothing is strong, nothing is holy: Increase and multiply upon us thy mercy; that, thou being our ruler and guide, we may so pass through things temporal, that we finally lose not the things eternal: Grant this, O heavenly Father, for Jesus Christ's sake.[5]

This was hardly the prayer of someone who had abandoned all belief in the transcendence of God or in a life beyond death.

The match between the *Honest to God* debate and the *God in Us* debate is not exact, but I believe that it does have sufficient parallels to allow my theological speculation. It is plausible to see Freeman as set on the same path (albeit more radically) as Robinson. Both showed a conviction that Christian faith today, if it is to be convincing in a sceptical age, must be expressed in secular terms. Both showed a radical scepticism themselves about traditional forms or expressions of Christian faith, being prepared to reduce them to considerable caricature. And both men appeared as evangelists, though radical evangelists: for them the way to commend Christian faith was to prune it of those features which no longer seemed plausible. Ramsey and Mascall dissented from all three strategies. They both believed that Robinson and others were deeply misleading and should be opposed. It seems reasonable to speculate that if they had been alive today they would have responded similarly to Freeman. But I think that their style of objection would have been very different.

Let us suppose for a moment that both Mascall and Ramsey are still alive . . .

First Mascall. Space does not allow me to cover all of the points that he makes against Anthony Freeman's *God in Us*. His response is almost three times as long as Freeman's eighty-seven pages – which he clearly does not hold in any high regard, as his title *Yet More Secularisation of Christianity* indicates. Instead, I can only present the bones of Macall's overall critique and a small part of his exegesis.

Thirty years after his devastating critique of Robinson and van Buren in *The Secularisation of Christianity*, Mascall argues that Feeman has confused the changing with the changeless and has himself become an instrument of promoting not Christian faith but secularization. While seeking to find modern terms in which to express the gospel, Freeman has actually jettisoned the heart of the gospel and capitulated to the modern world. Instead of challenging the modern world with the changeless truths of the gospel, he has in reality denied these truths using the very categories of the modern world. Secularity has been brought by Freeman into the centre of Christianity, reducing it simply to secularity.

For Mascall, this a clear example of a school of Protestant theology which he identified in the 1960s:

> [This theology] takes as its starting-point the outlook of contemporary secularised man and demands that the traditional faith of Christendom should be completely transformed in order to conform to it. . . . The general criticism to which this secularisation of the Christian faith exposes itself is that it reduces the dialogue between Christianity and contemporary thought to a purely one-way process; there is no question of contemporary thought adapting itself to the Gospel, the Gospel must come into line entirely with contemporary thought. Whatever demands the Gospel may make on contemporary man on the ethical level, on the intellectual level it embodies a policy of unconditional surrender by the Church to the world. This would be serious enough at any time, but

it is particularly deplorable at a time when, in our Western civilisation at least, the world is, in its outlook, radically irreligious. Indeed the proponents of the policy see in this fact its main recommendation. The contemporary man, they say in effect, is so radically secularised that he simply cannot accept supernatural Christianity; therefore we must completely de-supernaturalise Christianity in order to give him something he can accept ... a *soi-disant* 'Christianity' in which there is no such being as God, nobody survives bodily death, nobody hears us when we pray, there is no risen Saviour and nothing for us when we are dead.[6]

Mascall finds much in Anthony Freeman's *God in Us* to support this picture of a reduced Christianity which has capitulated to a secular and irreligious world. He notes that very early in the book Freeman insists that once God was thought to have 'direct and personal control, not only over the hearts of kings and queens, but over the whole physical universe'. But today, he asserts, 'we no longer live in a world where such an idea has any place' (p. 3). On the following page he claims even more bluntly that 'we no longer live in a world where God is understood as having that kind of control over events at all' (p. 4), and on the next that people today 'know with their brains that God does not interfere with our lives' (p. 5).

In the modern world Freeman believes that we should adopt a more radical form of Christianity which admits that 'religion is a purely human creation' (p. 9):

Radicals say that we do not need to bring in the supernatural at all. It belongs to that long-gone world of the past. It may have a place in fairy tales and horror films but it has no place in our understanding of the real world. All aspects of our life – physical, mental, aesthetic, moral, spiritual – all are human in origin and content. To invoke the supernatural is unnecessary, because we can explain all aspects of our life without it. It is also dangerous, because it leads to our claiming supernatural and indeed divine authority for things which are in truth only human. ... Today ... a number of people are finding meaning in a non-supernatural version of Christianity,

after they have given up belief in an objective personal God.
(p. 10)

To make his own position abundantly clear, Freeman
immediately adds, 'I am now among that number.' He goes
on to recount his 'conversion experience', as he terms it.
For him, 'once I was able to admit to the possibility that
I did not believe in God, wonderful things started to
happen' (p. 12). Mascall has always delighted in slightly
acid jokes – he adds at this point: 'wonderful things did
indeed start to happen.... Freeman was fortunately
deprived by his Diocese of his roles first as an advisor and
then as a priest.'

It is unnecessary to cite all the occasions on which Mascall notes that *God in Us* seeks to deny that supernatural
belief is a prerequisite for Christian faith. His case against
Freeman is that he continues to use Christian language
even when he has evacuated it of any traditional meaning
– in a mistaken desire to conform the gospel to modern
secularity. Freeman wishes to claim that 'I can still benefit
from using God religiously, without believing in him as an
objective and active supernatural person' (p. 24). He has
in reality, Mascall claims, retained the shell of Christian
faith and practice while evacuating it of any content. So,
when it comes to prayer, Freeman admits that 'I do not
actually believe that there is anyone "out there" listening
to me' (p. 52), and he is unambiguous that 'religious language does not describe things that actually exist "out
there"' (p. 81). Even the Bible is entirely humanized: 'the
Bible is a human writing, with no higher authority than we
choose to give it on its own merits.... I could just as well
make the same claim for Shakespeare's plays, Tolkien's
Lord of the Rings, or *Winnie the Pooh*' (p. 21). Not surprisingly, Mascall observes, sin is also seen by him purely as a
human invention (p. 30), as indeed are the Creeds (p. 39).
Even 'justice' suffers the same fate (p. 66).

Mascall notes a developing arrogance in Freeman. The
Preface to *God in Us* claims modestly that it is written by

one 'who does not aim to prove anything or defend anything, but rather to muse aloud for his own benefit and that of any who may care to eavesdrop' (p. vii). But as the book develops it soon becomes more polemical. Half-way through, the primary reason for adopting this radical version of Christianity emerges. It is quite simply that traditional beliefs 'are becoming impossible for many people to find any meaning in':

> Thousands of people in the church, and millions outside it, are looking for a new way to give meaning to our human lives. While the church clings to these outdated ways of speaking, it will be unable to speak to this generation. (p. 48)

Twenty pages later, his claims have become even more strident. The possibility of life beyond death is simply dismissed as 'no longer credible'. For good measure he adds: 'small wonder that people turn away from the church in their millions in their search for meaning. Traditional doctrine is thus the cause of the problem' (p. 68).

Of course, Mascall's analysis of Freeman's critique continues for many more pages – it sparkles with logic, jibes, biting wit and controlled anger, all which are impossible to reproduce here. He finds provocative and contentious claims on almost every page of *God in Us* – made typically on the basis of assertion and on the presumption that Christianity should be wholly conformed to the secular world, rather than on the basis of the world needing to be conformed to Christianity. Mascall argues that Freeman understands the role of the theologian exactly the wrong way around. Freeman as 'theologian' has surrendered unconditionally to the secular world. Secularization has triumphed.

However, there is another element in Mascall's analysis of *God in Us* which is worth noting. At certain points in the book Freeman makes positive claims about his new radical faith. Just as he was scornful of these positive elements in van Buren and Robinson in the 1960s, so

Mascall is thoroughly scornful of them in Freeman today. In all these writers he notes a tendency to depict their own views as 'authentic'. Each 'retains the classical phraseology of Christianity whilst entirely changing its meaning'.[7] He is also puzzled, especially by van Buren and Freeman who have both discounted any supernaturalist Christology, that they remain so firmly attached to Jesus. And all of them seem to use personal language to depict their faith – personal language, that is, which is drawn primarily or even solely from human beings – language about 'the depth of our being', about 'contagious freedom', or about 'God in us'. In Robinson's case, his 'peculiar interpretation of God as the Ground of being, and the ambiguity which he imports into that interpretation, might almost lead one to suspect that in his view it is a serious error to distinguish between the two commandments at all'.[8]

All these elements, so Mascall argues, feature strongly in *God in Us*. So, having admitted that he no longer believes in God in any traditional sense whatsoever, Freeman still wishes to claim that 'one of the things I found was that in a new way I could give real meaning to belief in God. That surely is authentic grace' (p. 12). And what, asks Mascall, is this new way which gives 'real' meaning and 'authentic' grace? Thirteen pages later it turns out to be simply this:

> Now I have decided to change my use of the term God. Instead of referring it to a supernatural being, I shall apply it to the sum of all my values and ideals in life. To describe my new God I must list those values. What are they? Some are positive things like goodness, love, power (rightly used), knowledge, wisdom, etc. and some are negative, such as freedom from the fear and tyranny of death, of suffering, etc. (p. 25).

Mascall is triumphant at this point. Freeman's new God is evidently anything that he chooses 'it' to be. The important thing about this God is that it is simply and solely 'my values and ideals in life'. Mascall argues that since he remains a nostalgic romantic Freeman 'chooses' to relate these values to Jesus and to the Bible – but of course he could (and might yet) choose to choose them differently. He still enjoys going to church, especially to a church which uses the BCP – since 'it gives me a place in a tradition' (p. 53) – and he still depicts himself as an 'authentic' Christian. But in reality this 'new, bracing, beliefless Christianity' (p. 58) is no more than the sum of his own 'values and ideals in life' and prayer is no more than 'aligning one's will and one's actions with one's highest values' (p. 57).

But why, asks an exasperated Mascall, call this Christianity? Surely it is nothing more than an idealistic secularism? Since Freeman's values are so self-consciously chosen they clearly could have been chosen differently. For example, they could have been Hitler's values which were so chosen. Hitler too was doubtless also concerned about 'aligning one's will and one's actions with one's highest values'. Of course, he was not too keen on the Churches – especially if they asserted biblically consonant values – but that was just his choice. Otherwise, he appears thoroughly commendable in Freeman's terms.

Mascall finishes with a waspish flourish. One could be forgiven for concluding that Freeman, like Robinson before him, 'had despaired of trying to convert the world to Christianity and had decided instead to convert Christianity to the world'.[9]

There was a polemicism about Mascall which belied his self-perception as a neo-Thomist. In some respects he was more like Augustine than Aquinas. A gentle, pious, considerate and ascetic person in private, he was a fierce and sometimes belligerent defender of the faith in print. Michael Ramsey, too, was a defender of the faith, but in quite a different manner.

George Carey's essay shows clearly how much Michael Ramsey agonized about his response to *Honest to God*. His *Image Old and New* was indeed 'a typical piece of Ramsey theology – wise, astute and inclusive'. He heeded Owen

Chadwick's warning 'to avoid any appearance of writing a counter pamphlet' and 'to take out as many references as possible to *Honest to God*'. Throughout he tried to say something positive about the debate before offering a wider corrective. To echo James Griffiss's essay, Michael Ramsey was indeed a truly 'Catholic' theologian. He wished to understand and even to learn from theological views which were not his own, while at the same time commending a generous and tolerant orthodoxy. He believed whole-heartedly that 'it has been a characteristic of our Anglican portion of the Holy Catholic Church to learn from episodes of human thought without becoming in bondage to them'.[10] Unlike Mascall, he did not believe that theologians such as Robinson 'were inventing theologies of compromise with the secular world; it was rather that they were trying to meet, often in clumsy and muddled ways, pressures and currents already moving powerfully in and beyond Christendom'.[11] Anselm remained one of his strongest mentors – 'faith seeking understanding' rather than 'faith demanding understanding'.

His new pamphlet, responding to the Freeman debate, is entitled *God in Us and Us in God*. Again I can only give a brief and inadequate account of this irenic and inclusive document. My summary is no substitute for the original.

Ramsey starts this new pamphlet with a long interpretation of Paul's sermon to the Athenians as told by Luke in Acts 17. First, he notes that Paul began this famous sermon not with a biblical text or even from a securely Christian premise but from the secular–pagan world of his audience. Paul immediately observes positively that 'I see that in everything that concerns religion you are uncommonly scrupulous.' He does not start by condemning or criticizing, but by trying to engage sympathetically with the secular world. Paul notices where there are promptings of faith, even in quite unexpected and apparently uncongenial places. This is the sermon of a great missionary reaching out beyond the emerging Church to people in the world at large. Ramsey insists that it is indeed right 'for us to be ready to find God not within the cosiness of our own piety but within the agony of the world and the meeting of person with person'.[12]

Ramsey's second observation about this sermon is that Paul attempts to expand his audience's understanding of God. Noting the proper mystery at the heart of the inscription 'To an unknown God', Paul tries to evoke in his hearers something of the majesty of the 'God who created the world and everything in it'. Paul argues that this God 'does not live in shrines made by men'. For Ramsey

> it is the putting of our own feeble little grasp of God, or our own individual picture of God, in place of God himself which is the peril of 'religion'.... Religion ... can mean a set of pious attitudes and practices within which we look for God, forgetting that God may *sometimes* be found less amongst them than amongst the things we call non-religious or secular.[13]

The third point that Ramsey draws from this celebrated sermon is that God is not to be reduced to our human level. This God is the creator not the creature, the one who 'created every race of men', who 'fixed the epochs of the history and the limits of their territory', the one in whom 'we live and move', the one in whom 'we exist'. This God is not to be reduced to anything simply 'shaped by human craftsmanship and design'. Ramsey uses this point to make an irenic point himself. In a remarkable passage he recognizes the aspirations of many people in the secular world:

> We need to see how and where 'religion' may be a thing far less than Christianity, far less than the living God, and often too far off from the hungry world in whose midst Christ is to be found. We need to see if there are some who are helped by thinking not about God above us in heaven, or even God around and near, but about the deep-down meaning of human life in terms of love. There may be those who find there the heart of the matter; and this *is* God, even though a man may not be able to cry with Thomas, 'My Lord and my God'.[14]

187

This passage in his interpretation of Paul is remarkable because it does not fully represent either Paul's position or Ramsey's own. For both of them God is more than this. Both do wish to affirm 'My Lord and my God'. Both wish finally to avoid confusing the creature with the creator. God indeed 'is not far from each one of us', and yet God is still not to be confused with us. Hence the title of Ramsey's new pamphlet, *God in Us and Us in God*.

The fourth and final point that Ramsey draws out from this sermon is that, despite his sceptical audience, Paul concludes with the resurrection. Paul has reached out and tried to learn from and identify with the Athenians, yet he finally preaches as a Christian. God has 'given assurance to all by raising [Jesus] from the dead'. Of course, this provokes some in the audience to scoff and others to patronize Paul. No matter. Paul cannot simply reinvent or refashion his faith to suit his audience. For Ramsey, this 'is what we have meant when we have spoken of "revelation" and of "grace": God finding us rather than we finding God . . . the imagery of revelation, the imagery of God beyond and within, within and beyond, Father, Son, Spirit'.[15]

This interpretation of Acts 17, which I am afraid I have shamefully compressed, occupies almost half of Michael Ramsey's new pamphlet. He remains, as John M. Court shows, committed to biblical theology. Only once this interpretation is complete does he turn to Anthony Freeman's *God in Us*. There are clearly many contentions and caricatures in the latter which must upset Ramsey as much as they do Mascall. However, this does not show at any point. He seems determined to avoid even the moderated amount of irritation that he expressed about John Robinson in 1963. He regretted that for years to come. Now he is determined to endorse some of the positive features of *God in Us* and gently to prod some of its obvious weaknesses. And he does all of this by returning to the four points that he has drawn from Acts 17.

On the first point he argues that Freeman is right to

attempt to engage with the secular in a serious way. His heart and missionary instincts are in the right place. Freeman is genuinely attempting to communicate the Gospel to a sceptical age. His anguish is genuine: 'Why is the Western world afflicted today by a sense of aimlessness? It is precisely because the old Christian hope, caricatured by opponents as, "pie in the sky when you die", no longer works for people'.[16] Yes, writes Ramsey, it is essential that the Church should be deeply concerned about the aimlessness of many people today and by the failure of Christians to reach them. We cannot simply expect a world that has drifted away from the Church readily to hear traditional ways of expressing Christian faith. These are real issues and it is possible that faith expressed in more worldly, and perhaps even more humanist, terms might be *one* way of reaching people.

At the same time, Ramsey believes that it is right to ask whether the world is quite so secular as Freeman presumes. There are still many signs of sacredness and the holy around us – in the values that many 'secular' people hold, in the resurgence of conservative forms of religious belonging, in the aspirations behind the New Age movement, in the persistence of private prayer, and so on. Of course, these can be exaggerated, but they do not easily fit the picture of a society presented by Freeman which can make no sense today of any supernatural claims or symbols. The Western world may be considerably more mixed and confused than Freeman presupposes. As a result, therefore, he may be offering the world a version of Christian faith which is so severely pruned of any supernatural elements that it cannot meet the tentative religious longings that are present in 'secular' society.

The second point that he draws from Acts 17 reminds Ramsey that Paul is seeking to start with his audience's tentative aspirations towards God and then to expand them. There are features of *God in Us* which seek to do just that. There are moments when Freeman seems to recognize that faith is not simply something invented or manufactured by human beings. It is in a real sense 'given'. 'My own view', writes Freeman, 'is that what I call genuine faith is not a thing we can choose. It has been called a gift. That is certainly what it feels like' (p. 24). Again, he writes a little earlier about his new theological position: 'One of the things I found was that in a new way I could give real meaning to belief in God. That, surely, is authentic Christian grace. That, surely, is the *gift* of faith' (p. 12).

However, the weakness of Freeman's position, Ramsey suggests gently, is that he appears to contradict this perception of 'grace' by insisting repeatedly that faith is simply a matter of personal and purely human choice. So having written so movingly about faith as grace and as 'not a thing we can choose', on the very next page he asserts: 'Now I have decided to change my use of the term God. Instead of referring it to a supernatural being, I shall apply it to the sum of all my values and ideals in life' (p. 25). The language of grace disappears, as does any concept of faith being the possession of the Catholic Church and not simply a matter of individual choice. Ever conscious that Christian faith is not simply the possession of Anglicans, let alone of individual radical Anglicans, Ramsey stresses that items of faith are never something that we simply 'choose'. Faith is properly faith when it involves a sense of being 'caught up' in the truth, of being prompted beyond ourselves and beyond our individual, rational wills. Faith as grace is indeed 'given', as Freeman sometimes – but sadly not always – recognizes.

This leads Ramsey naturally to his third point. The vision of Paul in Acts 17 is not simply of 'God in us' but rather of 'us in God . . . for in him we live and move, in him we exist'. There is a proper place in Christian faith, Ramsey insists, for talking about 'God in us'. The immanence of God, the presence of the Kingdom of God within us, the Incarnate Christ, are all vital parts of the gospel. Yet they are also balanced by the transcendence of God, the Kingdom of God which is 'not yet', the risen and ascended Christ. If it is sometimes a weakness of other-worldly forms of Christianity to forget about the first, it is very severe limitation of *God in Us* largely to ignore the latter. Both are essential features of a balanced and genuinely Catholic understanding of Christian faith.

Nowhere is this more evident than in prayer and worship. Ramsey is amused by Freeman's account of 'the former Archbishop of Canterbury' who replied to a journalist's question about the amount of time he spent on prayer each morning. 'One minute, but I spend fifty-nine minutes preparing for it,' was apparently his reply. Ramsey is clearly well used to people storing up (and perhaps improving) anecdotes about himself. Yet he finds Freeman's analysis of this anecdote too partial. Freeman writes:

> This was a good answer to an impertinent question, but in more friendly company the archbishop would surely not have denied the name prayer to this whole hour. To those with ears to hear the archbishop was getting as close as one dare in his position to saying, Christian prayer is not about talking to an invisible supernatural being. It is about stillness and recollection and aligning one's will and one's actions with one's highest values. (p. 57)

Well, up to a point – a fairly limited point, writes Ramsey – this is prayer and worship. But prayer and worship are also *very* much more than that. In one of his finest passages Ramsey explains:

> Within the worship of the Christians are acts of wonder at the beauty of God in the created world and his transcending holiness beyond it; and acts of gratitude for his costly redemption of mankind in Jesus. It is a worship in which sometimes the mind and the imagination dwell upon God's beauty and goodness, and sometimes mind and imagination enter the darkness as the unimaginable love of God is poured into the soul. It is a worship whereby the pain of the world is held upon the heart in God's presence, and the desires of men are turned towards the desire of God as we pray in the name of Jesus.[17]

Present within this quotation is Michael Ramsey's final point drawn from Acts 17. As an experienced priest and pastor he gently reminds Anthony Freeman that it is our privilege to be stewards of a rich and abundant faith. Throughout his long life he has stressed different parts of that faith at different moments and times – sometimes his stress was on the Incarnation, then it was on the resurrection, or the transfiguration, or the Holy Spirit, or increasingly in retirement upon prayer and worship. Christian faith is always more abundant than we can ever hope to comprehend, let alone express.

Some people express the hope that he, Michael Ramsey, might one day be able to write a 'systematic theology', a detailed and comprehensive account of Christian faith. Yet he has discovered that this is just a conceit. If faith is transformed into 'a system' or ever expressed in terms that claim to be 'comprehensive', 'fundamental', or even 'foundational', we can be sure that it is not the Christian faith in all its fullness. Even to begin to articulate their faith, Ramsey notes, the early Christians soon came to recognize that they needed four gospels and not just one. And Trinitarian theology instinctively recognizes that God is always beyond our limited understanding. If once we succeed in capturing God, even the 'God in us', we can be certain that the God of Jesus Christ has eluded us. He maintains that while 'renewal seems to demand the recovery of unities of understanding' it can in reality 'never be a tidy pattern which we can know and plan. Our wisdom as well as our folly faces the darkness of Calvary and the light of Easter.'[18]

As priests within the One, Holy, Catholic and Apostolic Church, Ramsey reminds Freeman, it is our privilege to seek to live within the faith, to commend the faith as imaginatively as we can to others, and to seek to understand the faith more deeply ourselves. It is not our role to prune the faith even if we thought that this might make it 'easier' for others to accept. We commend the faith only by living the faith and by living in the faith.

He ends his new pamphlet in the same way as he did thirty years earlier: 'But wherever we find him he is still the God who created us in his own image, and sent his Son to be our Saviour and to bring us to the vision of God in heaven.'[19]

It is time to end this speculation. The *Honest to God* debate which troubled Michael Ramsey so deeply has become a part of Church history. Yet the issues which divided John Robinson, Eric Mascall and Michael Ramsey remain. In a decade of evangelism we remain divided on how best to commend Christian faith to an age which ironically seems to be both sceptical and gullible. Perhaps these divisions can be represented as three broad and overlapping paths.

One path is to prune the faith, to remove from the Christian faith those elements which seem implausible to the modern world. A generation of theologians influenced by Bultmann and others was convinced that this was indeed the way to commend Christian faith to others. First demythologize Christian faith and then it can better be commended to a sceptical world. John Robinson, and more recently David Jenkins, seemed to be firmly set on this path. Anthony Freeman and Don Cupitt, set on removing transcendence altogether from Christian faith, are Robinson's more radical heirs. But perhaps this path over-estimates the single-minded scepticism of the 'modern age', and perhaps it also underestimates the damage that it can do to a Catholic and ecumenical faith.

Another path is simply to proclaim the faith. Some speak of 'confident evangelism' and see it as the business of the Christian to proclaim the clear set of propositions upon which Christianity is based. Others argue that, in the context of post-modernity and the breakdown of any common culture, it is the role of local communities to proclaim their faith to any who will listen. If the modern, or even post-modern, world cannot hear the gospel, then that is too bad for the world. Eric Mascall argued repeatedly that it was for the world to conform to the gospel, not for the gospel to conform to the world. The Gospel and Culture movement seems to be saying something very similar today – only once the categories of the Enlightenment are broken down, and people turn again to something like the categories that nurtured early Christianity, will a true return to faith be possible.

Michael Ramsey, I believe, represented a third path, which I have termed generous and tolerant orthodoxy. Unlike those who follow the second path, he remained suspicious until the end of seeing faith as 'a tidy pattern which we can know and plan'. He also believed that he had much to learn from the 'secular' world and from forms of theological expression which were not, and perhaps never would be, his own. In his earlier days, and especially in *From Gore to Temple*, he had looked for a single and distinctive pattern of Anglican theology and had failed to find one. For him orthodoxy meant living within the untidy edges of Christian faith. Unlike those who sought to prune faith in order to convince the modern world, he believed that even this form of 'tidiness' might destroy the complex balances that constituted a truly Catholic and ecumenical faith.

To use a concept which has strong currency today, Christian faith for Michael Ramsey was an ecosystem – far too rich and abundant for any single individual, or even denomination, to comprehend – an ecosystem in which one destroys individual parts (however strange) at risk of damaging the whole. The business of the Christian is to live within this ecosystem and gently to seek to draw others into its abundant riches. A generous and tolerant orthodoxy.

Notes

1. London: SCM Press, 1963.
2. London: SCM Press, 1993.

3. See Eric James, *A Life of Bishop John A. T. Robinson: Scholar, Pastor and Prophet* (London: Collins, and Grand Rapids, Mich.: Erdmans, 1987), ch. 7.

4. John A. T. Robinson, *Exploration in God* (London: SCM Press, 1967), p. 23.

5. The Collect for Trinity IV in the BCP: cited in James, op. cit., p. 312.

6. E. L. Mascall, *The Secularisation of Christianity* (London: Darton, Longman & Todd, 1965), pp. 6–7.

7. Mascall, op. cit., p. 84.

8. Ibid., p. 161.

9. Ibid., p. 109.

10. A. M. Ramsey, *Image Old and New* (London: SPCK, 1963), p. 15.

11. A. M. Ramsey, *God, Christ and the World* (London: SCM Press, 1969), p. 19.

12. *Image Old and New*, p. 15.

13. Ibid., pp. 3–4.

14. Ibid., p. 14.

15. Ibid., p. 8.

16. Freeman, op. cit., p. 67.

17. Michael Ramsey, *Be Still and Know* (London: Fount, 1982), p. 120.

18. Ibid., pp. 123–4.

19. *Image Old and New*, p. 15.

Index